More Praise for *Leading with Questions*

"Great leaders ask great questions. *Leading with Questions* has enabled our leaders at Sony Music to learn how to ask better and better questions. We are indeed a greater organization with greater leaders because of the powerful ideas in this book."

—Kathy Chalmers, executive vice president, Sony Music

"Marquardt presents a questioning technique that works and will enable leaders to grow from being good to being great."

—Lisa M. Toppin, financial services professional, New York Life

"How many books have forever changed your life? *Leading with Questions* forever changed my life and my leadership by shifting my focus from the burden of trying to have all the answers to the simplicity of only needing some of the right questions!"

—Bob Tiede, director, global operations leadership development, Cru, and blogger, leadingwithquestions.com

"In *Leading with Questions*, Michael Marquardt maps the future of leadership. 'The leader of the past was a person who told,' Peter Drucker once said. 'The leader of the future will be a person who asks.' Read this book if you want to see the future."

—Robert Kramer, chief learning officer, Centre for Leading Change, Brussels and Washington, DC

"I have learned that leadership is not about knowing all the answers. It's about knowing what great questions to ask, and carefully listening to those answers. This book is a timely piece of management wisdom that shows leaders how to ask great questions—questions that inspire, motivate, and empower the organization."

—Patrick Thng, managing director, Development Bank of Singapore

"This book skillfully bridges scholarly theory and down-to-earth common-sense tactics to provide a crystal clear guide to a very powerful leadership technique that changes people and organizations."

—Al D. McCready, chairman and CEO, McCready Manigold Ray & Co., Inc.

"*Leading with Questions* describes a very powerful and practical tool that has taken Constellation Power Generation into the top ranks of energy companies worldwide."

—Frank Andracchi, vice president, Constellation Energy Group

"Successful questioning is one of the most powerful skills, not just for leaders but for all people, and Mike has spent his career both studying the power of questions and asking questions effectively. This book captures the wisdom of his experiences."

—Keith M. Halperin, senior vice president, Personnel
Decisions International

"I have experienced the tools and techniques of *Leading with Questions* first-hand and highly recommend this book to new as well as experienced leaders. It has dramatically changed our leaders as they learn how to embrace Marquardt's questioning technique."

—Liz Cicco, training and development specialist, Bowne & Co., Inc.

"From the days of Socrates, our ability to ask the right questions has been revered as one of the greatest skills a person should possess when leading others. Marquardt's latest book is an invaluable 'how-to' resource for those intent upon finding solutions through reflective questioning."

—Eric Charoux, executive director, Charles Telfair Institute, Mauritius

"*Leading with Questions* is brilliant and thought-provoking. It is a huge wake-up call to all leaders that smarter questions are the best recipe for lasting success."

—Alastair Rylatt, author, *Winning the Knowledge Game: Smarter Learning for Business Excellence* and *Navigating the Frenzied World of Work*

"This book is a terrific guide and magnificent resource for those who wish to explore the power and benefits of leading with questions!"

—Dan Navarro, vice president and general manager, Pragmatics, Inc.

"*Leading with Questions* provides wonderful illumination on a subject often hidden in the shadows. In this book the genius of the author is his ability to capture the essence of what successful leaders do with questioning, and how they can use questions to change their lives and those around them for the better."

—Kenneth L. Murrell, professor of management and MIS, The University of West Florida, and author, *Empowering Employees*

"The ability to frame and ask the right question is a desired skill for everyone in life. *Leading with Questions* is a must-read book for those engaged in developing people to their maximum potential."

—Mohammed Effendy Rajab, director, Adult Resources, World Organization of the Scout Movement, World Scout Bureau, Geneva

"Marquardt has powerfully expressed how to reach the heart of effective leadership. This is a book not just to enhance existing leadership power but to develop everyone's latent leadership qualities."

—Francesco Sofo, University of Canberra, Australia, and author, *Six Myths of Critical Thinking*

"Marquardt has discovered the way to effectively lead the twenty-first century organization through questions and reflective learning. This book captures the essence of the questioning process and sets a practical basis for the long-sought-after learning organization!"

—Harry Lenderman, president, The Elk Forge Group; advisor, Sodexho University; and author, *Breaking the Educational Glass Ceiling*

"By focusing on the right questions, Mike Marquardt has peeled back the onion to reveal the true power of questions. This book shows leaders how to give their organizations the cutting edge that makes the difference between a good company and a great company."

—Bea Carson, president, Carson Consulting

"The ideas in *Leading with Questions* will provide leaders with new perspective on leading in the challenging twenty-first century."

—Lim Peng Soon, president, Learning & Performance Systems

"This is a must-read book! *Leading with Questions* will change the way you manage in your organization. This book is Marquardt's latest contribution to improving the way we work and communicate in our increasingly complicated world."

—Howard Schuman, managing director, Jodoh Investments LLC

"This book is the ideal guide for the corporate executive who would like to create a winning organization by asking the great questions."

—James Y. Lim, human resource manager, Arrow Asia Pac

"Leaders worldwide will be especially well served to master Marquardt's art of leading with questions!"

—Banu Golesorkhi, director, Research and Development, Pharos International

Leading

with

Questions

HOW LEADERS FIND THE RIGHT
SOLUTIONS BY KNOWING WHAT
TO ASK

Revised and Updated

Michael J. Marquardt

JB JOSSEY-BASS™
A Wiley Brand

Published by Jossey-Bass
A Wiley Brand
One Montgomery Street, Suite 1200, San Francisco, CA 94104-4594
www.josseybass.com

Jossey-Bass books and products are available through most bookstores. To contact Jossey-Bass directly call our Customer Care Department within the U.S. at 800-956-7739, outside the U.S. at 317-572-3986, or fax 317-572-4002.

Wiley publishes in a variety of print and electronic formats and by print-on-demand. Some material included with standard print versions of this book may not be included in e-books or in print-on-demand. If this book refers to media such as a CD or DVD that is not included in the version you purchased, you may download this material at **http://booksupport.wiley.com**. For more information about Wiley products, visit **www.wiley.com**.

Library of Congress Cataloging-in-Publication Data
Marquardt, Michael J.
 Leading with questions : how leaders find the right solutions by knowing what to ask / Michael J. Marquardt.—Revised and updated [edition].
   1 online resource.
 Includes bibliographical references and index.
 Description based on print version record and CIP data provided by publisher; resource not viewed.
  ISBN 978-1-118-83222-6 (pdf)—ISBN 978-1-118-83010-9 (epub)—ISBN 978-1-118-65813-0 (cloth) 1. Leadership. 2. Communication in management. 3. Questioning. I. Title.
 HD57.7
 658.4′5—dc23

                                                                    2013047036

eISBNs: (epub) 9781118795118, (epdf) 9781118795064

Printed in the United States of America
REVISED EDITION
HB Printing   10 9 8 7 6 5 4 3 2 1

Contents

Introduction   1

Part I   The Power of Questions

  1   An Underused Management Tool   11

  2   Benefits of a Questioning Culture   31

Part II   Asking Questions Effectively

  3   Why We Have Trouble with Questions   63

  4   Asking the Right Questions   83

  5   The Art of Asking Questions   103

  6   Creating a Questioning Culture   129

Part III   A Guide for Leaders on When and How to Ask
Powerful Questions

  7   Using Questions in Managing People   151

  8   Using Questions to Build Teams   177

  9   Using Questions to Solve Problems   199

10   Using Questions to Shape Strategy and Enable Change   213

Conclusion: Becoming a Questioning Leader   239

Resource A: Biographies of Leaders Interviewed   247

Resource B: Action Learning: A Powerful Training Program
    for Developing Questioning Leaders   255

Resource C: Resources for Training and Information on
    Questioning Leadership   271

Notes   275

Acknowledgments   283

About the Author   287

Index   291

To my mother, who taught me to love questions, and to my nine grandchildren, who love to ask questions of their grandpa

Leading

WITH

Questions

Revised and Updated

Introduction

Do you feel that people aren't providing the information you need? Do you wonder whether the people in your organization really understand your vision for where things need to go? Do you speculate about what your boss is really thinking?

Have you ever thought about getting all this information, and more, by asking questions?

Questions can elicit information, of course, but they can do much more. Astute leaders use questions to encourage full participation and teamwork, to spur innovation and outside-the-box thinking, to empower others, to build relationships with customers, to solve problems, and more. Recent research—and the experience of a growing number of organizations—now points to the conclusion that the most successful leaders lead with questions, and they use questions more frequently. Successful and effective leaders create the conditions and environment to ask and be asked questions. When the Center for Creative Leadership studied 191 successful executives, its researchers discovered that the key to the executives' success was creating opportunities to ask, and then asking questions.[1]

Consider these comments from among the successful leaders interviewed for this book:

- Chad Holliday, chairman of the board and CEO of DuPont: "I find that when someone engages me in a question, it wakes me up. I'm in a different place. Throughout the day, I try to do the same thing. I ask questions: I rarely make statements until I have sized up the person's energy and focus, and whether they are open-minded; only then can I move. If I don't ask questions, I could be underrating the situation and problem and miss the key issues."

- Pentti Sydänmaanlakka, former director of human resources at Nokia Networks: "Leading with questions has been always part of my leadership because I believe that leadership is not telling, but inspiring and showing others new places where they haven't been earlier."

- Isabel Rimanoczy, partner, Leadership in International Management: "I was working with pragmatic engineers who initially were upset that they were not able to get immediate answers and solutions to their questions. By focusing on questions rather than on answers, we inverted the process they were accustomed to. We put the focus on them, trusting their knowledge and wisdom. And, even when they did not think they had answers, they dived into themselves for the answers, and—not surprisingly—they always found the answers. . . . They had increased their self-awareness and realized that there was wisdom inside them that could be unearthed with questions."

• Robert Hoffman, executive director for organization development at Novartis: "Questions have changed me immensely. I have greater self-confidence and a more relaxed attitude. I don't feel that I always have to have the answers in conversations or in situations where I need to speak at the spur of the moment. I feel this has increased my communications skills, especially listening and persuading."

These leaders have discovered the amazing power of questions. Questions wake people up. They prompt new ideas. They show people new places, new ways of doing things. They help us admit that we don't know all the answers. They help us become more confident communicators. Unfortunately, many leaders are unaware of the amazing power of questions and how they can generate short-term results and long-term learning and success. If you have never considered making questions a tool in your leadership kit, this book is for you.

Of course, many leaders do ask questions constantly—questions such as these:

• Why are you behind schedule?
• Who isn't keeping up?
• What's the problem with this project?
• Whose idea was that?

Too often, we ask questions that disempower rather than empower our subordinates. These questions cast blame; they are not genuine requests for information.

Other sorts of questions are often no more than thinly veiled attempts at manipulation: Don't you agree with me on that? Aren't you a team player? If you tend to ask these sorts of questions, this book is for you.

So the point isn't that leaders just don't ask enough questions. Often, we don't ask the *right* questions. Or we don't ask questions in a way that will lead to honest and informative answers. Many of us don't know how to listen effectively to the answers to questions—and haven't established a climate in which asking questions is encouraged.

And that's where this book comes in. The purpose of *Leading with Questions* is to help you become a stronger leader by learning how to ask the right questions effectively, how to listen effectively, and how to create a climate in which asking questions becomes as natural as breathing.

RESEARCH ON LEADERS WHO LEAD WITH QUESTIONS

Over the past twenty-five years, I have been involved in research and developing leaders around the world, both as a professor and as a consultant and adviser to corporate executives. I have noted more and more frequently that leaders of the more successful companies tended to question others and themselves more often. I have sought to discover why questions are so important to leaders, why they result in such success, and what questions are the most powerful and used most frequently.

Who are some of the leaders who ask questions? And when and why did these leaders first begin using questions in their leadership work? What questions did they find to have been most powerful and successful? Why do these leaders ask questions, and what has been the impact of those questions on them and their organization? Over the past several years, I have asked individuals and audiences from around the world to identify leaders they believe use questions effectively. I then contacted professional colleagues who worked with leaders worldwide to identify leaders who both asked lots of questions in their work and were seen as successful leaders by their colleagues and subordinates. Occasionally the leaders I interviewed would refer me to another leader whom they saw as someone who also led with questions. I made an effort to get leaders from large and small companies, from public and private organizations, and from all parts of the world.

Among the many leaders who were identified, I interviewed a total of thirty from all over the world. I prepared the following list of questions to use in my interviews:

- When did you start using questions and why?
- What are some of the ways in which you use questions?
- What questions have been most effective?
- What has been the impact of leading through questions on your organization?
- How has the use of questions changed you as a leader?

Their responses to these questions and their stories are interwoven throughout this book.

Throughout the pages of this book, you will find the experiences of leaders who lead with questions—and the questions they ask. Among those who shared their experiences as questioning leaders are CEOs and top leaders from DuPont,

Alcoa, Novartis, and Cargill; public leaders from global and national agencies, as well as the political arena; and academic leaders at the secondary and college levels. They come from Brazil, Finland, Malaysia, Mauritius, Singapore, Korea, Australia, and Switzerland as well as North America. Brief biographies of these leaders are contained in Resource A.

Based on my quarter-century of experiences and interviews with scores of leaders who do indeed lead with questions, *Leading with Questions* provides a comprehensive foundation on ways to employ questions effectively when leading others. The book offers a variety of principles and strategies for asking questions as well as numerous stories of how leaders from every type of organization have used questions to attain organizational success and personal fulfillment.

KEY ASPECTS OF LEADING WITH QUESTIONS

This book is composed of three parts. In Part I, I explain why questions can be so powerful for individuals and organizations. Chapter 1 examines why leaders often prefer to provide answers rather than ask questions, and how limiting—and disastrous—that can be. I show why questioning is actually the ultimate leadership tool. Chapter 2 details the benefits, for leaders and organizations, of creating a question-friendly organizational culture. A questioning culture strengthens individual and organizational learning; it improves decision making, problem solving, and teamwork; promotes adaptability and acceptance of change; and helps empower people by strengthening self-awareness and self-confidence.

Part II offers practical guidance on asking questions effectively. Chapter 3 explains the stumbling blocks many of us face in asking questions and tells the stories of several leaders who have overcome them and benefited enormously. Chapter 4 shows how effective questions are empowering whereas ineffective questions disempower. It offers a thorough analysis of different types of questions, and it describes the roots of great questions. Chapter 5 explores the art of asking questions effectively, examining how one's attitude, mindset, pace, and timing all affect the impact of asking questions. As this chapter demonstrates, active listening and following up are integral parts of the art of asking questions. Chapter 6 turns from the personal level to the organizational, offering detailed advice on fostering an organizational culture that is conducive to questions.

Part III presents guidelines for leaders on using questions to achieve specific results for individuals, teams, and organizations. Chapter 7 discusses how leaders can use questions in managing their staff, strengthening relationships with direct reports, helping them to grow, and encouraging action and innovative thinking. This chapter also reviews the use of questions in orienting new staff, setting goals and objectives, conducting performance appraisals, and leading staff meetings, among other topics. Chapter 8 describes how leaders can use questions to improve team functioning, energize team meetings, solve problems, help teams overcome obstacles, and resolve conflict. Chapter 9 explores how and why questions can be effective in solving problems. Chapter 10 shows how questioning can strengthen entire organizations—sharpening strategy, vision, and values, and building the capacity for change—focusing on questions with both internal and external stakeholder groups. The Conclusion encourages the reader to begin the journey to becoming a questioning leader.

Three resources are included in the book. Resource A provides brief biographies of the thirty leaders who shared their experiences in asking questions. Resource B describes how action learning develops questioning skills with leaders. Finally, Resource C identifies organizations, training programs, and websites for developing questioning leaders.

A NEW LEVEL OF LEADERSHIP

Leaders who lead with questions will create a more humane workplace as well as a more successful business. Leaders who use questions can truly empower people and change organizations. Most leaders are unaware of the potential of questions and needlessly endure a fractious, pressure-filled existence. My hope is that readers will change their style of leading and be more easily successful and fulfilled as leaders.

There is no doubt that all of us, especially those of us who are leaders, need to ask more questions—questions that will assist in the development of individuals, teams, organizations, and ourselves. Questions have become essential for our success. Poor leaders rarely ask questions of themselves or others. Good leaders, on the other hand, ask many questions. Great leaders ask the great questions. And great questions can help you become a great leader!

PART I

The Power of Questions

An Underused Management Tool

We live in a fast-paced, demanding, results-oriented world. New technologies place vast quantities of information at our fingertips in nanoseconds. We want problems solved instantly, results yesterday, answers immediately. We are exhorted to forget "ready, aim, fire" and to shoot now and shoot again. Leaders are expected to be decisive, bold, charismatic, and visionary—to know all the answers even before others have thought of the questions.

Ironically, if we respond to these pressures—or believe the hype about visionary leaders so prominent in the business press—we risk sacrificing the very thing we need to lead effectively. When the people around us clamor for fast answers—sometimes, *any* answer—we need to be able to resist the impulse to provide solutions and instead learn to ask questions. Most leaders are unaware of the amazing power of questions—how they can generate short-term results and long-term learning and success. The problem is, we feel that we are supposed to have answers, not questions.

I interviewed leaders around the world about their use—or avoidance—of questions. This comment by Gidget Hopf, president and CEO of the Association for the Blind and Visually Impaired—Goodwill Industries, is typical: "I just automatically assumed that if someone was at my door with a problem, they expected me to solve it."

Hopf thought it was her job to provide answers. Then she realized that there was another way: "Through coaching I realized how disempowering this is, and how much more effective I could be by posing the question back to the individual with the problem. . . . What I came to realize is that solving others' problems is exhausting. It is much more effective to provide the opportunity for them to solve their own problems."

Unfortunately, from an early age we are discouraged from asking questions—especially challenging ones—be it at home, school, or church, as this is considered rude, inconsiderate, or intrusive. Thus we become fearful of asking any questions. As we ask fewer questions, we become ever less comfortable and competent in asking questions.

And then when we become leaders, we feel that it is important for us to have answers rather than questions. We feel that asking questions—or being unable to answer questions addressed to us—may show that we are somehow lacking as leaders. But this attitude leads to inertia. Consider what Jeff Carew, a vice president at Collectcorp, told me: "The easy way to lead, particularly if you are competent at your job, is to tell

people how to do things in the way you have been successful."
Usually, as Jeff has observed, people become successful either
through a very capable boss who taught them the ropes or
through their experiential learning that resulted in a successful
track record and steady career advancement.

Successful executives think they know the answers. "The
problem with this," Jeff noted, "is if you do not create and
maintain a working environment where you are always asking
questions of your employees and forcing them to think, then
you will probably never be any better tomorrow than you are
today. Yesterday's solutions will not solve tomorrow's problems.

"I learned that you need to get to a different level of thinking if you are going to tackle tomorrow's problems—and who
else is better to teach you how your environment is changing
than the managers on the floor or in the trenches?"

Like Jeff Carew, a growing number of leaders recognize
that their organization's success, if not its very survival, depends
on creating a learning organization, an organization that is able
to quickly adapt to the changing environment, where every
engagement becomes a learning opportunity, where learning
and business objectives are necessarily interlinked. The ability
to ask questions goes hand in hand with the ability to learn.
A learning organization is possible only if it has a culture that
encourages questions.

Gary Cohen, author of *Just Ask Leadership*, rightly observed
that it is not possible for leaders in the twenty-first century to be
a know-it-all, nor is it in their or the organization's best interest to try.[1] It is more important that leaders ask questions that
move others to action and answers. We should recognize that

13

the employees that work for you today probably know more than you do about their job. And as leaders move up the ranks of an organization, they will undoubtedly end up leading people who perform tasks that the leader will not understand. Mike Stice, CEO of Access Midstream Partners, said to me, "I need to continually ask questions to become part of the organization. Questions enable me to increase alignment, engagement, and accountability. And it is not simply asking more questions. It is asking more and *better* questions."

Do you ever feel defensive when people ask you questions? Do you ever hesitate to ask a question, fearing it may reveal ignorance or doubt? If so, you are closing off the free flow of information and ideas your organization needs and potentially undermining relationships with those around you. In fact, avoiding questions can cause serious harm—and even disaster.

WHAT HAPPENS WHEN LEADERS DO NOT ASK QUESTIONS

History is replete with tales of dire consequences experienced by leaders who did not ask questions. Recent disasters at Lehman Brothers, Barclays, WorldCom, Enron, and Arthur Andersen can be attributed to the lack of inquiring leaders. Historians who carefully examined the events and details behind the disasters of the *Titanic*, the *Challenger*, and the Bay of Pigs have determined a common thread: the inability or unwillingness of participants and leaders to raise questions about their concerns. Some group members were fearful that they were the only one who had a particular concern (when, in fact, it was later discovered that many people in the group had similar concerns). Others felt that their question had already been answered in the minds of other group members, and if they asked the question, it would be considered a dumb question, and they would be put down as being stupid or not going along with the group. Because people did not ask questions, people lost lives when the *Titanic* sank, when the *Challenger* crashed, when President Kennedy authorized a covert attack on the Bay of Pigs in Cuba.

Sinking of the *Titanic*

Why did the *Titanic* sink? When the luxury ship went down, on April 14, 1912, more than fifteen hundred passengers perished. Afterward, many questions were raised on both sides of the Atlantic. How could the allegedly unsinkable ship go down on its maiden voyage across the North Atlantic? What had gone wrong? Why couldn't the planner and builders have foreseen such a tragedy? Upon investigation, it was discovered that several of the planners and builders of the ship had indeed been concerned, though none of them had ever raised their concerns in the company of their colleagues. Why not? Because of their fear of appearing foolish by asking dumb questions. If no other "expert" seemed unsure about the structure and safety of the ship, then everything must be OK. Once the voyage was under way, many reports came in from nearby ships describing icebergs around them. "*Titanic* received many incoming messages warning of ice," Robert E. Mittelstaedt writes in *Will Your Next Mistake Be Fatal?*, "but there is no mention of her inquiring of others for updates or more information. What if someone was

15

curious enough to ask for more information from the ships in the area?"[2]

The Explosion of the *Challenger* Spacecraft

The Space Shuttle *Challenger* was launched on January 28, 1986, and exploded seventy-three seconds after liftoff. Much of the research into what went wrong with the *Challenger* launch focuses on the lack of communication between NASA, Morton Thiokol, Inc. (MTI), and the Marshall Space Center. MTI, the contractor responsible for the component that failed during the launch, depended on Marshall for the contract, and Marshall in turn depended on NASA for funding and support. Almost two years before the fatal launch, MTI became aware that there could be a problem with the O-ring, a sealing component that prevents hot gases from escaping the solid rocket booster and burning a hole in the fuel tank (the physical cause of the *Challenger* disaster). The engineers at MTI documented this problem and insisted that further testing needed to be done to determine the reliability of the O-ring. On further testing, they confirmed that the O-ring *was not* reliable, particularly when the temperature dropped below fifty-three degrees. Why then was the *Challenger* given the go to launch on January 28, 1986, when the temperature at launch time was thirty-six degrees, well below the safety margin? The people around the table were afraid to express their doubts or even to ask questions that they had determined, before entering the room that morning, that they would ask.

The 1961 Bay of Pigs Invasion

Fears of shattering the warm feelings of perceived unanimity—fears of rocking the boat—kept some of Kennedy's advisers from objecting to the Bay of Pigs plan before it was too late. "How could I have been so stupid?" President John F. Kennedy asked after the Bay of Pigs fiasco.

What happened? In 1961, CIA and military leaders wanted to use Cuban exiles to overthrow Fidel Castro. After lengthy consideration among his top advisers, Kennedy approved a covert invasion. Advance press reports alerted Castro to the threat. More than fourteen hundred invaders arrived at the *Bahía de Cochinos* (Bay of Pigs) to find themselves vastly outnumbered. Lacking air support, necessary ammunition, and an escape route, nearly twelve hundred surrendered. Others died. Top CIA leaders blamed Kennedy for not authorizing vital air strikes. Other CIA analysts fault the wishful thinking that the invasion would stimulate an uprising among Cuba's populace and military. Planners assumed the invaders could simply fade into the mountains for guerilla operations. Trouble was, eighty miles of swampland separated the bay from the mountains. The list goes on.

Groupthink is the term Irving Janis coined for this phenomenon: the kind of flawed group dynamics that lets bad ideas go unchallenged by questions and disagreement and that can sometimes yield disastrous outcomes.[3] Kennedy's top advisers were unwilling to challenge bad ideas because it might disturb perceived or desired group concurrence. Presidential adviser Arthur Schlesinger, for instance, presented serious objections to the invasion in a memorandum to the president, but suppressed his doubts at the team meetings. Attorney General Robert Kennedy privately admonished Schlesinger to support the president's decision to invade. At one crucial meeting, JFK called on each member for his vote for or against the invasion. Each member, that is, except Schlesinger—whom Kennedy knew to have serious concerns. Many members assumed that other members agreed with the invasion plan. Schlesinger later lamented, "In the months after the Bay of Pigs, I bitterly reproached myself for having kept so silent during those crucial discussions in the cabinet room." He continued, "I can only explain my failure to do more than raise a few timid questions by reporting that one's impulse to blow the whistle on this nonsense was simply undone by our inability to challenge one another and ask questions."[4] After that huge blunder, JFK revamped his decision-making process to encourage questions, dissent, and critical evaluation among his team.

DAY-TO-DAY DISASTER PREVENTION

Questions and a questioning attitude are not just important for avoiding historic disasters: they are also useful day in and day out for giving feedback, problem solving, strategic planning, resolving conflicts, team building, and more. When we avoid questions, all these activities suffer, even if that doesn't lead to disasters of historic proportions. Consider what Cindy Stewart, president and CEO of the Family Health Council of Central Pennsylvania, told me:

> One of the first jobs that I had was in a sewing factory. My job title was "floor girl," which was the assistant to the "floor lady"—no kidding! This job entitled moving work from one process to another to assure that none of the workers in your section were without work, and that specific garment lots would be completed by the deliverable date. It was not considered a management position. I distinctly remember overhearing the management team discussing a particular bottleneck that routinely occurred with this one style of nightgown. As they wrestled with solutions, none of which worked, I can clearly recall that I was thinking: "I wish they would ask me." Since I was the one that worked the closest to the problematic process, I felt I was in the best position to solve the problem. Of course, they never did ask me.

In avoiding questions, the management team at that sewing factory closed off a potentially important source of ideas and information, and their problem-solving ability suffered as a result. The experience left a lasting impression on Stewart:

> I think I made up my mind at that time that, if I were ever to be in a leadership position, I would never assume that having the title would mean that I had all the answers. Over my twenty-plus years in executive positions, I have come to realize that much of my success can be attributed to the fact that I believe in the capacity of the people who have worked with me. I truly think that the leader who tries to know it all and tells everyone what to do is doomed to failure.

FACING REALITY

No company can become great, Jim Collins tells us in *Good to Great*, without the ability to confront the "brutal facts of reality."[5] Consider the story of the Boston Red Sox. As is well known, the team's 2004 World Series win was long in coming. But in the 1940s the Red Sox were one of the dominant teams in baseball. Then in the 1950s the team went into a significant decline—attributed, in part, to racism. As other major league teams were widening their talent pools by recruiting black players, the Red Sox were slow to change. The team passed on hiring Jackie Robinson and Willie Mays, and it became the last major league team to recruit black players. Not until 1959 did a black player show up on the diamond in a Red Sox uniform. Prejudice played an obvious role. But reinforcing this prejudice was an unquestioning attitude. As Sidney Finkelstein writes in *Why Smart Executives Fail*, "Tom Yawkey, the owner of the Boston Red Sox, provides an all-too-typical example [of complacent prejudice]. When his scouts reported that African-American players were not good enough or simply not ready for big league play, he accepted their reports without question. Yet any serious attempt to verify these evaluations might have caused Yawkey to question his picture of baseball reality."[6] When leaders fail to ask questions, they forgo the opportunity to test their own assumptions and prejudices, whether those prejudices involve race or beliefs about consumer behavior, strategic threats, market conditions, product quality, staff abilities, or what have you.

The failure to ask questions, in other words, allows us to operate with a distorted sense of reality. In fact, in "Zombie

Businesses: How to Learn from Their Mistakes," Finkelstein calls companies that are unable to question their prevailing view of reality *zombies*. A zombie company, he says, is "a walking corpse that just doesn't yet know that it's dead—because this company has created an insulated culture that systematically excludes any information that could contradict its reigning picture of reality" (p. 25).[7] But as GE's former CEO Jack Welch says, leading successfully means "seeing the world the way it is, not the way we hope it will be or wish it to be."[8] Those responsible for the Bay of Pigs, the *Challenger* disaster, and the sinking of the *Titanic* were all operating under a distorted picture of reality because they failed to ask questions.

Organizations and leaders that avoid questions are actually losing opportunities to learn, according to Noel Tichy. "This is not a trivial issue. Many executives close off learning. In their day-to-day interactions with staff they are usually either issuing instructions or making judgments about the ideas or performance of others."[9] By telling rather than asking, Tichy says, they are actually making their organizations dumber, "less smart, less aligned, and less energized every day." In such organizations, "there is little or no knowledge transfer, intelligence is assumed to reside at the top, and everyone below senior management is expected to check their brains at the door."[10]

Mike Parker, president and CEO of Dow Chemical, notes, "A lot of bad leadership comes from an inability or unwillingness to ask questions. I have watched talented people—people with much higher IQs than mine—who have failed as leaders. They can talk brilliantly, with a great breadth of knowledge, but they're not very good at asking questions. So while they know a lot at a high level, they don't know what's going on way down in the system. Sometimes they are afraid of asking dumb questions, but what they don't realize is that the dumbest questions can be very powerful. They can unlock a conversation."[11]

QUESTIONS AS THE ULTIMATE LEADERSHIP TOOL

Many years ago, in his best-selling classic *How to Win Friends and Influence People*, Dale Carnegie noted that "an effective leader asks questions instead of giving orders." Oakley and Krug call questions the "ultimate empowerment tool" for the leader.[12] They observe that the better we as leaders become at asking effective questions and listening for the answers to those questions, the more consistently we and the people with whom we work can accomplish mutually satisfying objectives, be empowered, reduce resistance, and create a willingness to pursue innovative change.

John Kotter, the noted Harvard professor and author on leadership, writes that the key difference between leaders and managers is that leaders focus on getting to the right questions, whereas managers focus on finding solutions to those questions.[13] The focus on finding answers must not obscure the importance of asking the right questions. Successful leaders know that they cannot get the right answer without asking the right questions.

Peter Drucker found that effective executives all tended to follow the same nine practices:

- They asked, "What needs to be done?"
- They asked, "What is right for the enterprise?"

- They developed action plans.
- They took responsibility for decisions.
- They took responsibility for communicating.
- They were focused on opportunities rather than problems.
- They ran productive meetings.
- They thought and said "we" rather than "I."
- They listened first, spoke last![14]

Questions are at the heart of each of these practices.

The importance of asking questions was forcefully conveyed in 1843 when John Stuart Mill wrote *The System of Logic*, in which he noted the emptiness of a set of opinions accumulated without the help of strong-sense critical thinking. "He who knows only his side of the case knows little of that. His reasons may have been good, and no one may have been able to refute them. But if he is equally unable to refute the reasons on the opposite side, he has no ground for preferring with opinion."[15]

The ability to ask questions effectively is one of a leader's most important tools. Donald Peterson, former CEO of Ford Motor Company, once remarked, "Asking more of the right questions reduces the need to have all the answers."

In my own interviews with successful leaders, I found a similar willingness to express ignorance and an equal respect for the power of questions. Consider these remarks from Douglas Eden, president of Cargill's Malt Americas division:

> When I came back from my assignments overseas and was appointed president of Malt Americas, I was asked to make critical changes, as the business was failing. We

had to quickly decide whether to stay in or exit, and if we stayed in, what changes would be necessary to make the business viable. I did not consciously make a decision to become a questioning leader, but it began to naturally occur, as I had lots of questions and had to search for answers. Should we remain an efficient, low-cost supplier, or should we become the premier solution provider to the brewery business? What would be of most value to brew masters? Technical solutions such as better foam and flavor, or supply-chain solutions?

I was new to the brewer's malt business and naturally had lots of questions. Some of the staff wanted me to be more directive and to tell them how to execute various tasks. I really did not know immediately what to do and was not ready to immediately propose strategies. Some were more comfortable with this approach than others. As we all got better at asking questions of each other, we generated solutions that led to longer-term contracts and more value to our customers.

Now, four years later, we are a more successful business. I attribute much of this success to our ability to ask questions. Our business is very complex, and we have to search for the answers together.

Both these leaders were willing to say "I don't know" and to ask questions and work with others to find answers. As Collins tells us, "Leading from good to great does not mean coming up with answers and then motivating everyone to follow your messianic vision. It means having the humility to grasp the fact that you do not yet understand enough to have the answers and then to ask the questions that will lead to the best possible insights."[16]

Another example of a leader who makes effective use of questions is Commander D. Michael Abrashoff. Through what he calls "grassroots leadership," Commander Abrashoff turned around the operations of the USS *Benfold*, one of the U.S. Navy's most modern warships. His methods were not complex, yet the results were astounding. Under Abrashoff's twenty-month command, the *Benfold* operated on 75 percent of its allocated budget, returning $1.4 million to the Navy coffers. During that time, the ship's combat readiness indicators were the highest ever in the history of the Pacific Fleet. The promotion rate of his people was two and a half times the Navy average. The predeployment training cycle, which usually takes a total of fifty-two days, was completed by the *Benfold* crew in just nineteen days. During a twelve-month period under the previous command, there were twenty-eight disciplinary actions for which twenty-three sailors were discharged. During Abrashoff's tenure there were five disciplinary cases and no discharges. Under his predecessor thirty-one people were detached from the ship for limited duty, usually for complaints of bad backs. He had only two crew members leave for health reasons. On average, one third of all recruits don't make it through their first term of enlistment, and only 54 percent of sailors stay in the Navy after their second duty tour. Commander Abrashoff had 100 percent of the *Benfold*'s career sailors signing on for another tour. It is estimated that this retention alone saved the Navy $1.6 million in 1998.[17]

What did he do to stage such a turnaround in less than twenty months? As he himself remarks, he continuously asked questions; he listened, and then he acted on what he heard.

Almost immediately upon taking command, he had a fifteen- to twenty-minute personal interview with each of his staff of three hundred. He asked each person these three questions: "What do you like best about this ship? What do you like least? What would you change if you could?"

Abrashoff acted as quickly as he could to implement the ideas that came from these questions. He realized that simply following existing procedures and doing things the way they had always been done could no longer be effective.

Abrashoff set the vision and trusted his crew. He helped people take pride in their work.

> Whenever I didn't get the results I was looking for on the *Benfold*, I tried to look inward before flying off the handle. I also asked myself three questions each time: "Did I clearly articulate the goals I was trying to achieve? Did I give people the time and resources they needed to succeed? Did I give them enough training to get the job done properly?" Eighty percent of the time, I found that I was part of the problem and that, through my actions alone, I could have altered the outcome significantly.[18]

Abrashoff questioned every rule. He noted that when an officer or sailor came to him for approval or a signature on something, his first question was always, "Why do we do it this way?"

> If the answer was, "Because this is the way it's always been done," I would say, "That's not good enough. Find out if there is a better way to do this."

26

After a while, people began doing their homework before they ever brought issues to me. And they could explain, "This is why we do things this way." Or, "We've thought of a better way to get this accomplished." It drove my officers crazy, but by creating a culture in which we questioned everything, we were training our people to keep their eyes open to new ways of doing business.[19]

GREAT QUESTIONS DEFINE GREAT LEADERS

Asking rather than telling, questions rather than answers—this has become the key to leadership excellence and success in the twenty-first century. Peter Drucker, considered the leadership guru of the twentieth century, noted that the leader of the past may have been a person who knew how to tell, but certainly the leader of the future will be a person who knows how to ask. With the growing complexity and speed of change in the world, the traditional hierarchical model of leadership that worked yesterday will not work tomorrow. The leader simply won't know enough to adequately tell people what to do; the world is changing too rapidly. No one person can master all the data needed to address the complex issues that confront today's organizations.

Michael Dell, founder and leader of the computer company that bears his name, is a strong believer in the power of questions. "Asking lots of questions opens new doors to new ideas, which ultimately contributes to your competitive edge," he says.[20] Dell is also a big believer in learning from everyone in the company. He does this systematically by polling people around the company. "We also learn a lot by asking the same question in similar groups across the company and comparing the results. . . . If one team is having great success with medium-sized companies, we cross-pollinate their ideas . . . throughout the organization."[21]

Leaders need to create a questioning climate in which employees feel safe and able to trust the system and the people involved. Without this level of safety and comfort, people are generally unwilling to be vulnerable and to be comfortable answering questions that may seem threatening. And without trust and openness, people are unwilling to communicate about feelings and about problems, and thus ask the leader questions that might help them.

Marshall Goldsmith, recognized as one of the top leadership coaches, regularly teaches leaders to ask questions. In "Ask, Learn, Follow Up, and Grow," he writes,

> The effective leader of the future will consistently ask—to receive advice and to solicit new ideas. Tomorrow's leader will ask a variety of key stakeholders for ideas, opinions, and suggestions. Vital sources of information will include present and potential customers, suppliers, team members, cross-divisional peers, direct reports, managers, other members of the organization, researchers, and thought leaders. The leader will ask in a variety of ways: through leadership inventories, satisfaction surveys, phone calls, voice mail, e-mail, the Internet, satellite hookups, and in-person dialogue.[22]

Aside from the obvious benefit of gaining new ideas and insights, Goldsmith adds, "asking by top leaders has a secondary benefit that may be even more important. The leader who asks is providing a role model. Sincere asking demonstrates a willingness to learn, a desire to serve, and a humility that can be an inspiration for the entire organization."[23]

LOOKING AHEAD

Contrary to much received wisdom, effective leaders do not have all the answers; rather, effective leaders make it a practice to ask questions. One of the best things you can do to strengthen your leadership is to ask questions. Another is to encourage others to ask questions.

When we learn to ask questions and do so effectively, our questions can transform individuals, groups, and organizations. How this is so is the topic of the next chapter, which explains the many dividends that a question-friendly organizational culture pays.

QUESTIONS FOR REFLECTION

1. How can I use questions to be a more effective leader?
2. What problems have I created because I did not ask questions?
3. What are some of the great questions I have asked others?
4. What great questions have I been asked in my lifetime?
5. Am I able to say "I don't know"?
6. Of whom do I ask questions and why?
7. What questions can I ask to help the people around me to learn?

8. How can questions build a learning culture in my organization?

9. Have I encouraged others around me to ask questions?

10. How can I improve my skills in asking questions?

Benefits of a Questioning Culture

We have all heard sayings like these:

- Go along to get along.
- Don't rock the boat.
- They're not paying me enough to think.

If these and similar comments are commonplace around your organization, it is safe to say that it does not have a questioning culture. In organizations that discourage questions, information is usually hoarded, people keep their heads down and stick to their knitting, and few people are willing to take any risks. In answer-driven organizations, curiosity, risk taking, challenging the status quo, and even the willingness to be wrong all take a back seat.[1] The prevailing culture of such organizations, either implicitly or explicitly, calls for rigidity, risk avoidance, protectiveness, defensiveness, and automatic routines and habits. These organizations usually suffer from low morale, poor teamwork, and poor leadership. They become fossilized, even moribund.

Leaders, through questions, can build a culture in which questions are welcomed, assumptions are challenged, and new ways to solve problems are explored. Questions establish an inquiring culture in organizations, and such an inquiring culture builds a learning organization. Michael Dell, founder of Dell, Inc., observes that "Asking lots of questions opens new doors to new ideas, which ultimately contributes to your competitive edge .... That's why you must encourage the free flow of information at all levels."[2]

Questions also build a culture of accountability. They can foster commitment without barter and sustain the corporate community through civic engagement.[3] Jack Welch, in his book *Winning*, states that leaders must indeed be the ones who ask the most and the best questions.[4]

WHAT IS A QUESTIONING CULTURE?

When we ask questions of others and invite them to search for answers with us, we are not just sharing information; we are also sharing responsibility. A questioning culture is a culture in which responsibility is shared. And when responsibility is shared, ideas are shared, problems are shared (problems are not yours or mine, but ours), and ownership of results is shared. When an organization develops a questioning culture, it also creates a culture of we, rather than a culture of you versus me, or management versus employees.

Pentti Sydänmaanlakka, a former HR director at Nokia, outlines some of the qualities that a questioning culture generates:

> Leading with questions gives the opportunity for the subordinates to be more active. To be active, they need to learn the skill of self-leadership. Through questions, they will also take more responsibility and be more motivated and committed. People like the feeling that they have found the answer themselves. Leading with questions means that there is an atmosphere where you can challenge everything; questions create an open communications culture. Leading with questions for me personally has meant more freedom as a boss.

Kouzes and Posner emphasize the importance of leaders' engaging people throughout the organization in what they do and why they do it. They ask us to imagine how much more ownership of the values of the organization there would be when leaders actively involve a wide range of people in their development. "Shared values," they note, "are the result of listening, appreciating, building consensus and practicing conflict resolution. For people to understand the values and come to agree with them, they must participate in the process. Unity is forged, not forced."[5]

Questions asked by leaders transform the organization, as they can evoke the images of what employees hope to create, and of the values and behaviors desired by their people.

Leaders show, through the power of their questions and the words chosen within those questions, the means as well as the metaphors for organizational vision, values, attitudes, behaviors, structures, and concepts.

A questioning culture has six hallmarks. When an organization has a questioning culture, the people in it

- Are willing to admit, "I don't know."
- Go beyond allowing questions; they encourage questions.
- Are helped to develop the skills needed to ask questions in a positive way.
- Focus on asking empowering questions and avoid disempowering questions.
- Emphasize the process of asking questions and searching for answers rather than finding the "right" answers.
- Accept and reward risk taking.

ORGANIZATIONAL BENEFITS OF A QUESTIONING CULTURE

Questions serve as the foundation for increasing individual, team, and organizational learning. Every question can be a potential learning opportunity. As a matter of fact, deep and significant learning occurs only as a result of reflection, and reflection is not possible without a question—whether the question be from an external or internal source. A culture that encourages questions therefore is a culture that encourages learning. As Adams notes, "question-driven cultures have the capacity to respond swiftly and effectively to problems inside the organization while staying ahead of the curve in planning for external challenges and opportunities."[6] Organizations that ask questions will be more dynamic, agile, collaborative, and creative.

The act of questioning actually has an impact on the human brain. To demonstrate this, take a heading in this or any book and convert it into a question. For example, consider the statement "Action learning helps us to learn." If you simply ask yourself, "How does action learning help us to learn?" you will be surprised by how much more you will learn from that section—and how much of it you will retain.

Learning depends on curiosity and asking questions. The experience of curiosity is equivalent to continuously living and operating out of a question frame as simple as "What's this?"—as all children do. It is through questions that we operationalize curiosity into behavior, and as a result they are the foundation of any kind of learning, be it formal, informal, or personal.[7] Questions, especially challenging ones, cause us to think and to learn.

Jeff Carew, vice president of Collectcorp, explains the role of questions in organizational learning:

> Collectcorp is becoming more of a classroom. . . . Our working environment is one in which everyone is asking questions on how to make things work better. We are not looking for "the answer"; we are looking for better solutions than any one of us could come up with on our own.
>
> Yesterday's solutions will not solve tomorrow's problems. I learned that you need to get to a different level of thinking if you are going to tackle tomorrow's problems—and who else

is better to teach you how your environment is changing than the managers on the floor or in the trenches?

Carew highlights an important aspect of a questioning culture. A questioning culture promotes ongoing questions. The point is not to find the answer. Rather, in a questioning culture we keep asking and learning. We may come up with an answer today—and a better answer tomorrow. As Effendy Mohamed Rajab of the World Organization of the Scout Movement told me, "There is no such thing as the correct answer." Rajab says the point of asking questions is to gain perspective.

Mike Stice, CEO of Access Midstream Partners, an Oklahoma-based oil and gas company, told me how he has had a number of opportunities to use questions to understand and handle organizational disputes:

> The dispute is often between functional leads accountable for functional excellence and operational groups responsible for execution. Open-ended questions allow me to determine if the issue at hand is first and foremost a result of an unconfirmed bias or a real difference of opinion driven by differing priorities. Specific and direct questions allow both parties to uncover their own bias or differences and reach constructive compromises. It is especially rewarding when the questions lead to a breakthrough in relationships, which results in long-term benefits well beyond the current dispute at hand.

Mark Harper, president of Wholesale Marketing for ConocoPhillips Petroleum, stresses that gaining new perspectives is one of the most important uses of questions. He says he uses questions to encourage people "to see things from a different perspective." And he adds, "Surfacing and changing unconscious biases is very important." When we open our eyes and minds to the perspective of others, we open ourselves to learning.

Adams observes that the "smartest, most innovative and productive organizations, and the most talented leaders and managers, are successful not because they have quick answers but because they create inquiring cultures. Such environments are highly thoughtful and strategic, fostering the most innovations and breakthroughs in products, services, and even operations."[8]

Vance Coffman, former chairman and CEO of Lockheed Martin, comments that he built a learning organization by asking questions. "Great questions are good fuel for fostering curiosity. Great questions guide my search for common sense explanations of a situation." When asked, "What critical questions should a new senior executive at Lockheed Martin ask," he replied: "Why is this the way it is? Do we understand why we got there?" He continued:

> Good questions make better programs or get us out of problems, whatever the circumstances are. If people on your team value what's important, why it's important, and what's the logic that drives us to do this versus that, then you've got a pretty good team. Once I'm comfortable with the way a team's decision process works and how the team members work together, that team will solve problems and deliver terrific results. But if a team isn't functioning well, I first ask

why and then how can we change it to get better players in the right jobs at the right time. When the right players are in place, a solid team can be honest enough, curious enough, and interested enough to push each other on why our company is doing this, how it got there, and where it is going. Essentially, I want two sharpened edges in a team: critical inquiry combined with collaborative action.[9]

In fact, inquiry and collaborative action naturally go together. It is hard to collaborate with others without asking and answering questions. And asking and answering questions in a positive way naturally leads to collaboration.

Improved Decision Making and Problem Solving

As a questioning culture promotes learning, it also helps improve decision making and problem solving. Questioning helps people gain perspective and understand the perspectives of others. As they see issues and problems from different points of view, they gain an appreciation for their complexity—and also expand the range of possible solutions. When I interviewed David Smyk, a partner with Executive Healthcare, he highlighted the value of perspective in decision making and problem solving:

> It has been my experience that people who are immersed in a project often do not readily see the possible solutions that lie beyond their comfort zone of knowledge. As a questioner, I can help increase their vision by challenging them to define issues in ways that are new to them. These

38

generally open-ended questions are nonthreatening, and when a person does not feel they are "on the spot," the flow of creative thinking can be accelerated. In addition, the proper framing of questions makes it easy to view the questioner as a team member who can assist in achieving a successful outcome, and not as an obstacle to the process.

Organizations that encourage leaders at all levels to take the time to ask thoughtful and probing questions improve the odds of making good decisions. When you talk to the people closest to the problem, you can gather more relevant information, gain a better perspective, and be able to act more confidently than if you relied solely on your own resources, opinions, and perceptions. As Bobb Biehl, president of Masterplanning Group International, notes, "If you ask profound questions . . . you get profound answers. If you ask shallow questions, you get shallow answers. If you ask no questions, you get no answers at all."

By their nature, questions help us to think clearly, logically, and strategically. Questions increase communications and listening as well as prevent us from misjudging each other's motivation. We can find the truth more easily through listening to each other's questions than by being forced to listen to opinions and statements that are based on assumptions. Truth emerges not from opinions but from the free movement of open minds. Questioning causes us to view one another as resources.

Questions encourage and enable individuals and groups to understand, to clarify, and to open up new avenues of exploration for solving the problem. They provide new insights and ideas for strategic actions and potential paths for solutions. Questions and responses to those questions provide necessary and valuable information to solve problems faster and make better decisions. They give leaders the opportunity to gain unfiltered information. Through questions, leaders seek to learn not only what directly causes the problem or what solutions may work (which is single-loop learning), but also to seek to discover and learn what might be the underlying causes and solutions (double-loop learning) as well as the culture and mindset that create these causes and solutions (triple-loop learning).

Mark Harper of ConocoPhillips points to another benefit of a questioning culture: it helps create "a higher level of trust that dialogue and debate will occur before major decisions are made." As a result, he says, people feel included in the process and "there is more of a commitment to execution when changes have to be implemented."

Questions also generate alignment with a shared focus and make it more likely that you will solve the right problem. In *Smart Thinking for Crazy Times*, Ian Mitroff observes that individuals and organizations run into trouble because they too often solve the wrong problem.[10] Organizational psychologists such as Block[11] and Vaill[12] note that the problem originally presented is rarely the most critical problem for the group to work on; often it is only a symptom, and as the group works on it, a more urgent and important problem emerges. Leaders thus need to recognize that problem solving begins by first diverging through the use of inquiry, and only then using questions that create the converging and narrowing focus.

Too often, leaders assume that they have a clear picture of the problem. The obvious (but not always practiced) first step in solving any problem is first to be sure you know what the problem is. Most of us presuppose, because we have heard about or experienced the problem, that we now know and understand exactly what the problem is. And, even more dangerously, we believe that everyone else now has the same perception and understanding of the problem. In reality, if seven people experience the same problem, they will probably come up with seven different descriptions of what the problem is.

A questioning culture helps to undercut these typical and erroneous assumptions. When questions are routine and habitual, different perspectives will be highlighted naturally, and a fuller picture of the problem will result. The group will be more able to gain the big-picture perspective of the problem and a fuller understanding of the entire range of possible solutions before determining goals and specific strategies. The acquisition of a wide, helicopter view of the problem can be accomplished only by openly and freshly questioning each other and then reflecting on the responses. A central aspect of the reflective inquiry process is to encourage people to ask "dumb" questions—or, more accurately, fresh questions.

Greater Adaptability and Acceptance of Organizational Change

Change brings new ideas, new ways of doing things to the organization. In organizations without a questioning culture, change and new ideas are often rejected because they might conflict with existing, established mental models or ways of doing things, which have never been questioned. When questions are rare, those promoting new ideas have the task of confronting these existing assumptions without invoking defensiveness or anger. This is difficult to do in organizations where the prevailing culture discourages questions. Their questions, no matter how gently phrased, stand out and seem disruptive because questions are so rare. When an organization develops a questioning culture, however, questions cease to be unusual, cease to be threatening. This makes it easier for even difficult and challenging questions to be addressed—and for the organization to adapt to change.

When faced with change, people focus on what they are going to lose. The more people feel that they make a difference, the better they will feel about what they are doing. The better they feel about what they are doing, the more their self-esteem is enhanced and the more contributions they will make. By posing the right questions and engaging staff in the pursuit of a response, effective leaders gain more than just buy-in to the change. Effective leaders serve as the catalyst for change and give their followers the opportunity to exert some control in determining their future. Questions will enable staff to become more aware of how they contribute to the organization's goals, and thereby generate greater commitment to those goals.

Great questions cause the questioner to become more aware of the need for change, and to be more open and willing to change. The questions themselves may actually cause the leader to become a change catalyst. The leader who leads with questions will more likely champion new ideas heard and developed in the course of inquiry. New ideas and perspectives enable the leader to make strong arguments for advocating change.

Motivating and Empowering Employees

Good questions energize people. And a questioning culture can energize an entire organization. Margaret Wheatley notes how questions and the resulting reflection nourish people and develop internal motivation.[13] Questions create the conditions that foster openness and release energy. People are energized when they are questioned, because they have been asked for their ideas.

"Asking questions is fun," Doug Eden says. "Employees enjoy it." Eden is president of Cargill's Malt Americas unit. He began his career with Cargill in 1978 as a staff accountant in Minneapolis and served in senior management positions in Thailand and Australia as well as eight cities in the United States before becoming president. Asking questions, he says, "leads to meaningful dialogue, gets everyone involved, and actually provides me more credibility as a leader."

Blanchard remarks that too many leaders try to make people feel unimportant.[14] The important thing about leadership is not what happens when you're there but what happens when you are not there. Leaders who promote a questioning culture in their organizations move people from dependence to independence. Blanchard notes that great questions equip people, so that positive things happen when you are not there. Questions create a supportive, creative environment. By asking questions, leaders help people discover for themselves what is important for them in doing what is necessary for the organization. This discovery process improves their self-confidence and self-esteem, empowering them in the process. Concurrently, they take ownership of the solution because they have participated in developing it.

Questions can certainly empower and motivate people more effectively than exhortatory statements do. When leaders encourage a questioning culture, they put out subtle messages that build their people's self-esteem and self-confidence, which is a key to shifting their thinking paradigm. This message—"I care about what you think, and your opinion is important and it counts around here"—motivates people and builds positive attitude as well as enhances their personal satisfaction.

Good questions empower people to devise their own solutions. When people discover their own answers, they develop self-responsibility and accept ownership of the results. Asking people questions shows them that you value them. Questions move people from dependence to independence.

Stronger Teamwork

Putting people together around a conference table doesn't make them into a team whose members all pull together. Sue Whitt, global head of Pharmaceutical Regulatory Operations at Abbott Labs, previously served as senior vice president for Pfizer's global R&D business. She explained to me how she encouraged a questioning culture to bring her team together when she was at Pfizer:

> When I directed the integration for development operation at Pfizer, I had an integration team staffed with ten people from different segments. Staff meetings used to be very "ungrouplike." Everyone was constantly talking over each other, debating who's the smartest. It was difficult to get the group back to the goal of the meeting. Questions I asked began to change my group.
>
> I would ask about data. "Are you aware of how many databases need to be done by the end of the year? Would you like to prioritize? If so, on what basis, and how should we reprioritize?" At the end of each session, we asked questions such as "What worked and what went well? What could we do better?" We would then be sure to incorporate these ideas into our next session. I have continued to use this approach in my group meetings.

The people on any team possess an array of knowledge, wisdom, creativity, and energy. Leaders can best access this wealth of experience and empower their people by encouraging questions as a natural part of team discussions. Mike Coleman, vice president of the Alcoa Rigid Packaging business unit in Knoxville, Tennessee, told me that questions were critical in building his team:

> Alcoa was in a bad position and needed a turnaround when I first joined the company. The company needed a turnaround team. By asking lots of questions with different individuals, I was able to find and develop such a team.

I asked them what the problems were, what were possible solutions, how to handle internal and external problems, how to exist and move forward. I looked for responses like "Here's my vision—what do you think?"

Questions such as the ones Sue Whitt and Mike Coleman asked can generate an atmosphere of friendly collegiality. Questions help the group recognize and reorganize its collective knowledge. As group members engage in asking questions of one another, they gradually gain a group consensus on answers and strategies, as they now see each other's perspectives more clearly and also gain greater clarity of their own.

Questions, when asked at the right time in the right way, provide the glue that brings the group together and holds it together. Questions build strong and cohesive teams because of the many positive effects of questions on a group of people. Questions serve as models of responsiveness, helpfulness, and cooperation. An interesting phenomenon occurs as we ask questions about someone else's problem. The questioning process causes us to become more interested in that person's problem. And when we listen to someone respond to our question, we appreciate their efforts and their attention.

Margaret Wheatley notes that leaders need to build more time for relationships and social time with teams.[15] When leaders question, they show respect, listening, and caring. They help the group achieve group goal clarity—a most essential element for building the team. Questions enable leaders to develop closer relationships among people. They demonstrate the questioner's ability to empathize and care about others.

Enhanced Innovation

Creativity requires asking questions for which an answer is not already known. The truth is that innovation is rarely the product of pure inspiration, that "Eureka!" moment when some genius comes up with a wholly new idea. Rather, innovation happens when people see things differently. It starts with a questioning culture that helps people gain new perspective and see things differently. Innovation is generated by great questions in an environment that encourages questions.

Pentti Sydänmaanlakka sees a questioning culture as an important foundation for innovation. "When my employees learned that I will not give answers at the beginning, but that I will first ask questions, then they learn to ask questions themselves and find solutions alone. They start questioning when they are alone." When you encourage such questions, Sydänmaanlakka says, you "create an environment which supports innovation, creativity, and a real spirit of curiosity."

Similarly, Collectcorp's Jeff Carew says that when he began to create a questioning environment in his department, new ideas blossomed:

> What resulted was something better than what was happening before I changed my leadership style. We came up with new alternatives, ones that I had not thought of. My direct reports felt a greater sense of ownership to the ideas because they belonged in part or sometimes in whole to them—and most importantly, production in my area improved. And I grew as a leader; some of the best ideas were coming from new managers because they had a fresh perspective on the environment or their situation.

Questions can also encourage people to take risks—and risks are the precursors to most of the great ideas of history. For every step forward, someone had to wonder whether a current situation could be changed or made better. Questions needed to be asked: What could happen if I did this? Is there any other way to think about this? What possibilities exist that I haven't thought of yet? For example, Columbus could have asked himself, "Is there a sea route to India?" Or Picasso, when moving to cubism, "In what other ways could I depict the human form?"[16]

INDIVIDUAL BENEFITS OF A QUESTIONING CULTURE

Many of the organizational benefits just discussed also directly benefit individuals. For example, while the organization benefits from the results produced by motivated and empowered employees, those people benefit from the same results, of course, and also from the sense of well-being generated by that level of involvement in their work. Individuals also benefit from improved learning, greater decision-making and problem-solving abilities, and so on. Still other benefits of a questioning culture accrue primarily to individuals and only secondarily to the organizations of which they are members.

Greater Self-Awareness

Vaill points out that today's managers need a high aptitude for self-reflection and self-awareness as well as for action.[17] Astute and clear understanding of personal motives is one of the most critical of all leadership skills. Reflective questioners, according to Vaill, become better leaders. A questioning culture encourages reflection. When we feel free to ask questions and are open to the questions of others, it heightens our need to reflect. And as we are called on to reflect more, we become more natural at it.

Goldberg observes that most people are totally unaware of and unconscious about the internal questions they ask themselves—even though such inquiries virtually program their thoughts, feelings, actions, and outcomes.[18] Most of us are simply unaware of how important or pervasive our questions are to our way of thinking and acting. However, it is these very questions that serve as the basis for how we view life and make our decisions. When we are immersed in a culture that encourages questions, it helps us become more self-aware, more conscious of choices we have made, and more deliberate about our decisions.

Self-reflection enables us to better understand ourselves, gaining insight into why we do some things and avoid doing other things. For example, asking the question "Is this really worth my effort at this time?" helps you to reflect on priorities and values. How you respond can enable you to focus on what you can do to change the things you want to change. A question such as "Can you share with me why this particular issue bothers you so much?" helps you learn what is important to those around you. Questions enable you to better understand relationships in terms of how others perceive you.

People who consciously self-reflect are much more attuned to their inner feelings than those who don't, and thus likelier to recognize how these feelings affect them. Reflection helps us to become more attuned to our values, more candid and authentic, and better able to speak openly about our emotions. We also become more aware of our limitations and strengths, and therefore have a more accurate self-image.

Greater Self-Confidence, Openness, and Flexibility

Organizational cultures that encourage curiosity and questions help people develop themselves. People who ask questions have more self-confidence, as they see the people they question show appreciation and respect for the question and the questioner. When a nonthreatening environment for questions is a daily reality, people become ever more comfortable with themselves, know their strengths better, and are more self-assured. As leaders see their peers and their staff demonstrate greater capability and responsibility in responding to questions and taking more initiative, they can be more relaxed and flexible.

In organizations that discourage questions, on the other hand, questions and those who ask them may be seen as threatening. And when questions are not responded to openly or honestly, or are actually rejected, those who ask them can feel put down and marginalized.

Questioning cultures, by generating self-confidence, also tend to encourage adaptability in meeting new challenges. People who are comfortable with questions are nimble in adjusting to fluid change and limber in their thinking in the face of new data or realities. They can juggle demands without losing focus or energy. They are comfortable with ambiguity. Questioning leaders are likely to remain calm and clear-headed under high stress or during a crisis, and to remain unflappable when confronted by trying situations.

Robert Hoffman, executive director of human resources and organizational development at Novartis, highlights this aspect of a questioning culture:

> Questions have changed me immensely. I have greater self-confidence and a more relaxed attitude. I don't feel that I always have to have the answers in conversations or in situations where I need to speak at the spur of the moment. I feel this has increased my communication skills, especially listening and persuading.
>
> I have more trust in myself and others. Leading with questions has led to more trust, which appears to be a paradox of group life. I have stronger initiative and commitment.
>
> I learn more as I have become more directional by more questions. I have more patience and self-control, have greater openness and transparency. I now see myself as more adaptable and flexible. I am optimistic about opportunities [and] more inspirational and have greater vision and cognitive capability.
>
> Questions have given me greater understanding of organizational and political realities; I recognize the importance of organizational context and orientation. I am more willing to take risks in creating opportunities. I have a greater empathy with employees, customers, and others and a stronger commitment to develop others. My empowerment orientation is greater.

Bertrand Russell, the noted English mathematician and philosopher, once remarked that it was "a healthy thing now and then to hang a question mark on things you have long taken for granted." Leaders at all levels who question others and are able to accept questions exhibit a desire and ease in learning and improving themselves. They become more open to constructive feedback and criticism. Such leaders are more comfortable in asking people how they can better lead as well as what new leadership strengths they should cultivate.

Better Listening and Communication

When organizations develop a questioning culture, they help leaders at all levels become more empathetic and more in tune with their colleagues. People who are comfortable with asking and being asked questions have an increased ability to listen attentively and can more easily grasp the other person's perspective. Such leaders are able to get along more sensitively with people of diverse backgrounds or from other cultures. Those who lead with questions become less concerned about strict control and trust their people more. This freedom enables them to listen better and communicate in a more effective manner.

"Questions have made me sit back and be a better listener," Cargill's Douglas Eden says. "I am now much more comfortable with other people; I can more easily take an active interest in what people are saying. Questions have made my meetings more focused and effective, and have generated more solutions. I can more quickly get to the key issues."

The questions themselves force leaders to listen. Because followers see the questioning leader as more empathetic, they are willing to question and listen themselves; they hear more closely and are thus more willing to support initiatives and ideas from the leader.

Questioning leaders are adept at being persuasive and engaging when they address a group. Even when disturbing news or concerns arise, the leaders who question can retain the confidence and support of the organization. When leaders listen carefully to the answers given to their questions, the people around them appreciate their efforts and attention.

Better Conflict Management

Questioning leaders become better at managing conflict, because their solid questioning skills enable them to draw out all parties, understand the differing perspectives, and then find a common ideal that everyone can endorse.[19] Hii discovered that questioning leaders are more comfortable than their unquestioning peers with surfacing conflict, acknowledging the feelings and views of all sides, and then redirecting the energy toward a shared idea. They move toward a collaborative style of conflict management as opposed to being either overassertive or passive and withdrawn in their approach to conflict.

Because it is generally easier to confront others and be up-front with questions rather than with statements, organizations that encourage a questioning culture help people discuss issues and share concerns that otherwise might be kept hidden. Questions allow you to keep your opinions or perspectives in abeyance until you sense the interests or opinions of others.

Frank Andracchi is vice president for Constellation Generation Group. He told me how the use of questions helped him resolve serious conflict on at least two separate occasions:

> I have started to use questions in all phases of my business environment: during conversations, meetings, telephone calls, and even during the reading of documents. This process was most powerful in recent negotiations of a contract modification between Constellation and United States Steel. These negotiations were going in circles for a year before using the right questions as the vehicle to find the solution. Through the use of questions, the real issues were placed on the table and joint resolution to those issues agreed to, with both sides happy with the results.
>
> [Another set of] sites had developed a classic McCoys-versus-Hatfields attitude, causing a significant divide between the employees. This divide placed the project at risk of failure. Since the introduction of the use of questions to discuss the roots of the differences between the employees, the division has disappeared. Since this business unit discovered the use of questions, the four sites have increased to their highest level of cooperation to date.

In *Leading Quietly*, Badaracco notes that restraint is the precondition for finding creative solutions to difficult problems.[20] It requires that your whole mind grapple with what is really going on and what can be done. Questions enable leaders to understand and apply the essence of what Badaracco calls "quiet leadership."

Greater Understanding and Skills in Organizational and Political Realities

Questioning leaders tend to have more organizational awareness than their unquestioning peers; their use of questions makes them more politically astute and better able to detect crucial networks. Questions also help leaders read and understand key power relationships. They tap into what's happening and appreciate how people feel about issues and direction in the organization. Questioning leaders know what it takes to have greater control over their organization's destiny.

In *Leading Quietly*, Badaracco comments that "creative solutions to difficult political problems rarely spring full-blown into managers' heads."[21] Far more often, they result from a long effort to understand, shape, and take advantage of an ever-evolving and often surprising stream of events that can be seen only through the use of questions.

Effendy Mohamed Rajab says that asking questions has helped him to become more politically sensitive: "I don't expect to get the correct answer from any single line of questioning. The correct answer is highly dependent on the context and situations from political and cultural perspectives."

Leaders improve their ability to search the unfamiliar through the use of questions. Dilworth notes how questions provide a person with leadership skills that encourage fresh thinking, and thus enable us to "avoid responding to today's problems with yesterday's solutions while tomorrow's challenges engulf us." Questions provide leaders with the opportunity to take "appropriate levels of responsibility in discovering how to develop themselves."[22]

Stronger Commitment to Learn and Develop

Questions not only demonstrate a greater commitment to developing others but also make you more adept at cultivating others' abilities as well as your own. Leaders who ask questions develop their emotional intelligence through questions. Questioning leaders thus improve their ability to teach, mentor, and coach.

In the process of questioning to help others learn, the leader is more likely to become a devoted learner too, someone who takes time to learn and demonstrates a love for learning, who has become more clearly aware of the importance of creating great thinkers and learners throughout the organization. Through questions, people know more what leaders expect of them and are therefore more committed to learn. Through questions, colleagues know better how to set challenging but achievable goals and recognize the importance of continuous learning.

Sue Whitt of Abbott Laboratories says, "Questions have helped me learn. I loved to learn and learned a lot through questions. Questioning is a style I am comfortable with. I do not feel that I need to know everything. That's why I hired all these talented people. My joy is to deal with challenges outside my comfort zone. Questions help me to defuse tensions and to build people who enjoy working with each other."

John Morris observes that only through constant questioning do we see more clearly just who we really are and what remarkable resources we have access to. We will also see more clearly what is really facing us, and we will become more capable of accepting and responding to change.[23]

Stronger Leadership

Jim Collins, in his best-selling classic *Good to Great*, reports his discovery that leaders of great companies are both very humble and very persistent.[24] In his description of "Level 5 leaders," he observes that the successful leaders of the companies he studied recognized that the title of leader does not make one a source of all wisdom. Great leaders are humbled by the realization of all they do not know. They know that asking questions of a few will not give them enough data; to succeed, they must make asking questions of anyone and everyone their top priority.

According to research done by Joseph Badaracco, leaders who ask questions become more modest, a hallmark of Collins's Level 5 leader.[25] Questioning leaders are realists and don't inflate the importance of their own efforts. They take the time to drill down into problems by asking questions. Questioning leaders recognize that everyone is needed, and that everyone should serve one another, if the organization is to be successful.

Mark Thornhill, CEO of the Midwest Region of the American Red Cross, says, "Questions have had a significant impact on me. I now see that a true leader stands behind the follower; he is someone who is accessible to and supportive of the followers. I now lead more quietly. In reading Collins's book *Good to Great*, I learned that what great leaders do better than anyone else is question both internal and external customers."

To recap what Pentti Sydänmaanlakka told me, a questioning culture helps people "learn the skill of self-leadership." In other words, questioning helps develop leaders at all levels. Through questions, as Sydänmaanlakka said, people "will also take more responsibility and be more motivated and committed."

LOOKING AHEAD

In a 2006 interview with *Time* magazine, Eric Schmidt, then CEO of Google, remarked, "We run this company by questions, not by answers."[26] Given the benefits of a questioning culture, how should you go about creating one? This is the topic of this chapter's final questions for reflection. To pave the way, I first show how you can clear away some of the obstacles that hinder your ability to ask questions. The next chapter describes the various kinds of useful questions and shows why not all questions are useful. I then discuss how individuals can best ask questions. And finally, I discuss how the whole organization can be imbued with a questioning culture that empowers everyone.

QUESTIONS FOR REFLECTION

1. What is a questioning culture?
2. What are the benefits of a questioning culture?
3. How can I create a questioning culture?
4. What are some strategies and actions I can take to build a culture in which questions are welcomed, assumptions are challenged, and new ways to solve problems are explored?

5. How can I build trust, enthusiasm, and commitment through questions?

6. What questions can I use to empower my colleagues and employees?

7. How can I use questions to build greater self-awareness and self-confidence in myself and in others?

8. What are some ways that I can demonstrate openness and flexibility with questions?

9. How can I become a better communicator and listener through the use of questions?

10. How can I more effectively handle conflicts by asking questions?

PART II

Asking Questions Effectively

Why We Have Trouble with Questions

Remember Cindy Stewart's story from Chapter 1? As the "floor girl" in a sewing factory, she heard the factory managers discussing a bottleneck in the production line. "As they wrestled with solutions, none of which worked, I can clearly recall that I was thinking, 'I wish they would ask me.'" Unfortunately, many of us can see something of ourselves in those managers. They were having problems, their solutions didn't work, and they still didn't reach out to others with questions.

If, as noted in Chapter 2, the open inquiry represented by the free flow of honest questions and conversation is so powerful and beneficial, the question naturally arises: Why do we so often have trouble asking questions? In discussing this with leaders around the world, I have found that a number of answers come up consistently. We have difficulty with questions for four primary reasons:

- We avoid questions out of a natural desire to protect ourselves.
- We are too often in a rush.
- We often lack skills in asking or answering questions due to a lack of experiences and opportunities, of training, and of role models.
- We find ourselves in corporate cultures and working environments that discourage questions, especially those that challenge existing assumptions and policies.

OUR DESIRE TO PROTECT OURSELVES

One of the most difficult challenges you may have as a leader is to accept that you may not know what is right, or best, for most situations. We have become accustomed to having the right answers, so it's hard to let go of the answer-providing habit. We want to protect our self-image and our image in the eyes of others; we also want to protect ourselves from uncomfortable feelings such as fear. Exposing ourselves with questions offers risks on all these fronts. But people rarely start out this way. Asking questions is a natural part of our biological makeup. Ask any parent of a child under the age of three about how children love to ask questions. Unfortunately, most of us are told by our parents, teachers, and bosses to stop asking questions. Not only are we told not to ask questions, but when we do ask a question not considered appropriate or correct, we are ridiculed. As a result, we become afraid to ask questions. We begin to think that smart people do not need to ask questions, as they already have the answers. We protect ourselves from being perceived as stupid by not asking questions.

So when we become leaders, we of course want to be the one with the answers rather than the one with questions. As Cindy Stewart, now president and CEO of a successful nonprofit organization, told me, "After all, we have been socialized to know the answers." Asking questions or being unable to answer questions addressed to us may show that we are unprepared to be a leader. We fear being asked questions, as it may feel like an inquisition or interrogation. We have already, so many times in life, experienced the fear of not having the right answer and not looking good that it's easy to succumb to the temptation to avoid such situations in the future. Semler believes that managers overrate knowing where they are going, understanding what business they are in, and defining their mission.[1] This is a macho, militaristic, and self-deluding posture. Having the courage to give up control in exchange for freedom, creativity, and inspired adaptation should be the preference of the questioning leader.

Fear inhibits us from asking questions in another way. We sometimes fear that if we ask a question we will get an answer we do not like, one that depicts us as part of the problem, or one that indicates that a favored project has gone off course. When we ask questions that we truly do not know the answers to, we may get answers that cause us to change our mind or force us into an action we would prefer not to take. It is a natural human tendency to push potentially unwelcome information away. Thus

65

we avoid asking questions, especially when the answers may be threatening. Mike Coleman, vice president of Alcoa's Rigid Packaging business unit, says, "Those who have the inability to ask questions have problems with their ego."

or self-differentiate The antidote to fear is, of course, courage. Courage is always an act, not a thought. You cannot think your way into courage; you act your way into courage. Asking questions is not always easy, especially tough follow-up questions or questions that require deep and intensive soul-searching. A leader needs to be courageous and authentic and not intimidated by the rank or expertise or character of the person to whom the question is posed.

Courage includes the willingness to ask questions that may challenge—or even break up—current perceptions and patterns. Change also requires "challenging and altering old patterns and perceptions, for this is the very condition that allows something new to emerge."[2] Courage is required, because to keep looking for better answers, we have to be willing to give up our current beliefs or positions. Some answers are more accurate, appropriate, and useful or moral than others. For you to want to do the hard work necessary to find better answers, you need substantial curiosity and courage. As Block noted, it is lonely to get to the future first.[3] It entails a large responsibility. But if leaders are not willing to do it with courageous questions, that future may not materialize.

Occasionally there will be times when we must be able to challenge assumptions and beliefs in thinking and communicating—including our own. Inquiring leaders have to be able to acknowledge what they don't know and to ask provocative and inspiring questions. We don't listen to someone's argument with a blank slate. We feel a sense of ownership about opinions we call our own. It often takes incredible courage to give up on an opinion we have held for some time after listening to someone else. As critical thinkers, we have to struggle to force ourselves to try out new answers. The interplay between our old answers and new ones provides a basis for our growth.

Too often, when we encounter a question, we already have an answer. But sometimes we must ask questions whose answer we do *not* know. This takes courage, because asking questions and admitting we don't know an answer are behaviors not expected from leaders. We must have the willingness and courage to practice "not knowing." Leaders must be willing to "not know" or "not be right." If you are hesitant to ask questions whose answers may threaten you, consider the words of Suzanne Milchling, head of the Homeland Defense Business Unit in the Department of Defense: "It is the question not asked that gets me in trouble."

Feeling unable to risk and being fearful of asking questions traps many leaders into a cycle of inaction, defending intentions, and interpreting or explaining away others' perceptions. A well-thought-out defense or series of explanations and statements allows leaders to protect their ideal self-image. By staying focused on that image, however, leaders are prevented from seeing themselves as others do. This myopic view gets in the way of exploring others' perceptions, and the leader becomes locked in a self-fulfilling cycle of good intentions fueling behavior that may or may not lead to optimal results.[4]

Fear generally makes the leader focus on the followers and make sure that if results are not achieved, it is the followers' problem. Rarely does the leader's risk-averse focus leave room to turn inward and explore "What can I do differently?" or "How am I contributing to this situation?" The lack of information keeps such leaders in the dark and creates confusion for the rest, who may in turn decide to work around the leaders or withdraw to pursue their own objectives outside the leaders' reach. A leader who is willing to take risks will ask the questions that need to be asked.

WE ARE TOO OFTEN IN A RUSH

People become leaders in organizations for many reasons, but one of the primary reasons is that they build track records as problem solvers and being able to get results. This builds a pattern of behavior in which we are too focused on fixing problems right away so that we can check them off our to-do list and move on. Chad Holliday, chairman and CEO of DuPont, points to this sort of impatience as a reason some executives have trouble with questions. "It requires self-discipline to keep questioning," he says. "There is a great temptation to make statements, especially when you are in a hurry and want to do things quickly. This morning, I discovered that something should have been done two weeks ago. My first reaction was to tell them to 'get it done.'" But, he adds, he managed to resist this impulse and instead ask what happened and why. "I get better results this way," he says. Too often, leaders lack the self-discipline Holliday displayed.

When we use questions, we should be sharing not just information but also responsibility. Rather than telling people what to do, the leader must have the courage to ask them what needs to be done and then make a serious attempt to remove any obstacles in the way. This not only generates the best ideas but also gives people a stake in the success of an effort. If you want people to be there for the crash landing, you'd better invite them to the launch.

Few practical necessities are more obvious and critical than the need to get perspective in the midst of action. We all get swept up in the action, particularly when it becomes intense or personal. Self-reflection does not come naturally. Charles Ostland, principal of Oakton High School, says, "I found that in terms of leadership, I must personally work hard to become more reflective and ask more questions of people in an attempt to help them clarify their own opinion and position on an issue, rather than providing my own opinion or answer." Like many leaders, he says he has a "natural tendency to jump to a quick answer or give an initial opinion about something" before asking others for their views and solutions.

Asking the right question is not an easy task, especially when the group is struggling with an overwhelming problem or fighting alligators. Asking questions can take more time, especially as you are searching for new ideas. Most of us feel more comfortable in efficiently making statements and providing answers. We do not have the discipline or commitment to make time for questions. Asking questions, especially fresh questions, is hard work. But as Revans notes, "The capacity to ask fresh questions in conditions of ignorance, risk, and confusion, when nobody knows what to do next" is at the heart of great leadership.[5]

David Rock, director of the NeuroLeadership Institute, observes that leaders seek quick answers and innovative insights in short periods of time. Unfortunately, insights don't always happen so fast. His research has shown that creative outside-the-box inspirations do not arise under hectic conditions. David told me that

> An open mind is a quiet mind. Insights tend to involve connections between a number of neurons. An insight is often a long-forgotten memory or a combination of memories—memories that don't have a lot of neurons involved in holding them together. In other words, insights are made up of weaker, less noticeable connections. And because we have millions of neurons constantly speaking to each other, we only notice the louder of the signals. So, insights are more likely when you can look inside yourself and not focus on the outside world. When you feel safe enough to "reflect" on deeper thoughts and not worry about what's going on around you for a moment.

When leaders in an organizational context hit speed bumps that must be resolved, most of us tend to do almost the exact opposite of what the brain needs. We tend to put pressure on ourselves, or have that extra dose of caffeine, or gather more resources—or, worse, we brainstorm as a group, which creates a lot of mental noise. Our brains get so loud that we can't even hear ourselves think. Bosses accidently make employees less

70

efficient and creative all the time because they are unaware of the way people work most productively. David concludes that a better approach to thinking as a collective unit is to first define the question as a group. Then ask individuals to take time out and do something interesting but repetitive and simple for a while, and allow the unconscious brain to do the solving for you. David shared with me that in his work with organizations, he has "generated a 100 to 500 percent improvement in [the] manager's ability to solve complex problems with their teams, by teaching them about insight and giving them some models to practice with."

Leaders must maintain the capacity for reflection, even in the fog of war. This capability is similar to the ability of great athletes who can at once play the game and observe it as a whole—what may be referred to as "contemplation in action." Heifetz and Linsky note that a big-picture leader needs to "get on the balcony," to notice the various patterns that are occurring.[6] Being temporarily above the hustle and bustle of the crowd is important, to take the mental action of stepping back in the midst of all the activity and asking, What's really going on here?

The ability to do critical thinking and ask critical questions that can lead to clarity, precision, and accuracy is the sign of a leader who is concerned with truly making a difference and not just going for a quick fix. "In the final analysis, I learned that there is no such thing as the correct answers; it is only perspective," Effendy Mohamed Rajab told me. Rajab, the senior training and development director for the World Organization of the Scout Movement in Geneva, Switzerland, said that questions should be "designed to understand any issue from the perspectives of the respondents, but not necessarily the correct answers. Simply put, if you don't ask, you don't know for sure why things happen the way they happen."

LACK OF SKILLS IN ASKING QUESTIONS

We are all born with the ability to ask questions. When we are infants, even before we can speak with words, our subconscious naturally and continuously asks two questions whenever we make a sound or a movement: (1) what am I doing well (relative to learning how to walk and how to talk)? (2) what can I do better?

And when we can verbalize our thoughts, we love to ask questions of the people around us (ask any parent with a two-year-old). "What is this? Why? Why not? Where?" To the point that parents begin to tell their child, "Stop asking so many questions!" And as young children we hear this admonition from others around us—teachers, older children, relatives. So we stop asking questions and begin losing a most important skill of life.

Now I am a grandfather, and as such I consider it my most important role to undo the damage that my children do my grandchildren—namely, discouraging them from asking questions. Whenever I see one of my nine grandchildren, I say to them, "I love questions! You can ask me any question you want." And they do: "Why is your beard white? Why don't the clouds fall? Why can't we?" Of course, they love to have Grandpa around to share their joy of questions.

But the unfortunate fact is that many of us no longer have this ability to ask questions, for the simple reason that we are out of practice (not having practiced since the age of three when our parents told us to stop asking so many questions). We may have received thousands of hours of teaching in classrooms and training in the workplace on history, mathematics, computers, diversity, and leadership, but never anything on the asking of questions. The asking of questions, especially how to ask great questions, has never appeared in any of our curricula or on any of our performance appraisals. We have never gotten feedback on the quality of our questions. And rarely have we had a boss who was a model of an inquiring leader—someone who could demonstrate the skill, power, and benefit of questions.

Mark Harper, president of wholesale marketing for ConocoPhillips Petroleum, says that it took a while for him to gain skill in using questions as a management tool: "At the beginning it was uncomfortable and frustrating. I didn't know how to ask good questions. I had a tendency to ask too many leading questions, or I only asked questions when I knew I had to make a decision."

As Harper's comment demonstrates, even when we do ask questions, we find the process uncomfortable and frustrating. Too often, when we ask questions, we provoke defensiveness. We ask what we think is a simple question, such as "Why did that happen?" and people react as if we were accusing them of dereliction of duty. Or we ask an innocent question about a decision the boss has made, and the boss reacts angrily, as if to a direct challenge. In other words, even when we do ask questions, we do not do so skillfully, in a way that elicits a frank but friendly response.

When we lack questioning skills, all too often our questions are limited, incorrect, or simplistic. Ineffective questions lead to detours, missed goals, and costly mistakes. Goldberg notes that depending on how the leader asks a question, it can be perceived as "an invitation, a request, or a missile."[7] Because questions are so powerful and can be provocative and challenging, we must be skilled in their use.[8]

Asking good questions requires two critical skills. First, you must know what questions to ask, for questions are not all created equal. Second, you must know how to ask them. Chapters 4 and 5 offer guidelines on how to ask the right questions effectively.

CORPORATE CULTURES CAN DISCOURAGE QUESTIONS

Our environment or culture determines a large part of our personal behavior. For example, I behave very differently in a church than I do at a football game—same person but totally different behavior in different contexts. Likewise, I behave differently as a father than I do when I am with former college roommates—same person but in very different roles. Thus some of us may feel much more comfortable asking our child a question than we ever could asking our boss a question.

In some corporate cultures and with some bosses, it would be taboo and dangerous to ask too many questions, especially questions that might rock the boat or cause someone to lose face.

Thus we become afraid to question authority. In addition to corporate cultures and expected roles for those cultures,

Americans live in a national culture that, as Yankelovich and many cultural anthropologists have noted, "rushes to action."[9] In the face of any problem, we Americans tend to say, "What are we going to do about it?" We perceive thinking and reflecting as unproductive use of time (even though we admire a person such as Einstein, who would frequently be found in his office at Princeton staring into space).

And many corporate cultures have an aversion to listening to any news that isn't good. As Sidney Finkelstein writes in *Why Smart Executives Fail*, "It's especially easy for executives to accept good news unquestioningly and to investigate further only when there seems to be a problem. Enron, World-Com, and a long list of dot-coms all had corporate boards that refrained from questioning their policies or even looking too closely at what they were doing, because their stock prices were soaring" (p. 200).[10] When the board refuses to ask questions, that sends a powerful signal throughout the organization for people to keep their heads down.

Often new ideas are not welcomed or acknowledged in an organization because they might conflict with existing, established mental models or ways of doing things. Questioning leaders have the task of confronting these assumptions without evoking defensiveness or anger. They must be able to surface and test the mental models and basic assumptions of colleagues. Asking questions that are challenging requires risk, occasional conflict, and instability, because addressing the issues that lie beneath problems may involve upending deep and entrenched norms. Questioning leaders are confident and willing to challenge beliefs and assumptions.

Pam Iorio, former two-term mayor of Tampa, Florida, is a political leader who was able to ask questions, and served as a model questioner for others. As leader of a city of over three hundred thousand people, she developed a reputation for managing crisis and uniting adversaries. Pam left office with a remarkable 87 percent approval rating. Pam described to me how questions help her to succeed in her very challenging role.

> When I first became mayor, I was so excited about the many possibilities associated with the position that I talked too much. In meetings I expressed all kinds of thoughts and ideas—and the rest of the group wouldn't talk much at all. One day I asked my chief of staff what the problem was, and he said, "Your position is too powerful, so when you talk it stops others from expressing themselves." And so began the revelation that leadership was really about listening. It was a process for me, and there are still times when I say too much. But now when I enter into a situation where people are coming to the table with different points of view, I start by asking myself, "What is most important to the other person?"

Pam noted that when she listened carefully, she was able to "pick up on the one thing that is important to the other side." This helped her in framing her questions; it also helped her become more aware of what's negotiable and what's not, as well as ending a meeting with everyone feeling good about at least something.

Leaders must continuously look for "white-space opportunities"—that is, new areas of growth possibilities that often fall between the cracks because they don't naturally match the skills of existing business units. They look for "strategic intent"—that is, a tangible corporate goal or destiny that represents a stretch for the organization. For example, at Walmart everyone is encouraged to look for things that don't seem right and ask questions. It is called "ETDT: eliminate the dumb things."

Heifetz and Linsky note that people expect leaders to provide them with right answers, not confront them with disturbing questions and difficult choices.[11] That's why the initial challenge and risk of exercising leadership is to go beyond your authority—to put your credibility and position on the line in order to tackle the problems at hand. Without the willingness to challenge people's expectations of you, there is no way you can escape being dominated by the social system and its inherent limits.

Chapter 6 explains how you can build a questioning culture in your team and organization.

CONFRONTING OUR DISCOMFORT WITH QUESTIONS

This combination of fear, time pressure, lack of skills, and a discouraging corporate culture all result in many leaders asking relatively few questions, and often asking questions only out of a sense of desperation. But, as the leaders I interviewed for this book show, it doesn't have to be that way.

Take Frank Andracchi, vice president of Constellation Generation Group, an energy company. He told me:

I have started to use questions in all phases of my business environment: during conversations, meetings, telephone calls, and even during the reading of documents. Personally, I have found that since using questions—or, more correctly stated, as I listen to any conversation and think of questions to obtain more information—I learn more, know more, and improve my comprehension. Additionally, as an executive, I find I interfere significantly less during any meeting or conversation. The "brain switch" to thinking of questions has been extremely powerful, taking my leadership up another step.

And Jeff Carew, vice president of collections for Collectcorp, has also made the transition from telling to asking:

I discovered that I was leading by telling rather than teaching—or by giving answers not asking questions—after a 360-degree leadership evaluation program.... This feedback initiated a change in the way I managed my staff. Now I refuse to give the answer to problems; I ask questions of them on how to make things better in their area, or how to approach something differently. At first they were skeptical but eventually got with the program.

Collectcorp is becoming more of a classroom, where I am a facilitator for my group rather than the guy in the corner who will give you the answer to everything.

I am making a bigger impact in my team's growth. And their confidence is growing because they know the answer to their problems is in their heads. My job is to help them get it out.

Many executives told me that the simple act of asking questions has brought about profound change. For example, Robert Hoffman, executive director for organization development at Novartis, whom I quoted in Chapter 2, is worth repeating here:

> Questions have given me greater understanding of organizational and political realities; I recognize the importance of organizational context and orientation. I am more willing to take risks in creating opportunities. I have a greater empathy with employees, customers, and others and a stronger commitment to develop others. My empowerment orientation is greater.

Another leader who experienced personal growth from adopting a questioning leadership style is Tom Laughlin, president of Caravela, an international leadership and team development consulting firm:

> Questions have made an absolute difference to me as a leader. I don't have to have all the answers anymore. It has caused me to think differently. I have gone from trying to find solutions to often superficial symptoms to now getting to the real problem. I am actually a better problem solver because I am a better problem identifier.
>
> Questions have made me a better coach and mentor. Questions allow me to check out my sense of where I am and should be. They allow me to express my emotion and intuition and understanding. People think more highly of me. People feel more encouraged.

When we learn to use questions, not only do we experience personal growth, but we also help our whole team. Says Suzanne Milchling: "I use questions so as to get buy-in so that all are on the same page. Questions allow us to have a common understanding and to make us think of all the steps in the process. . . . By asking questions of yourself and others, you are able to round out the understanding of the situation for all."

Author John Morris remarks that only "through constant questioning do we see more clearly just who we really are, and what remarkable resources we have access to. We will also see more clearly what is really facing us, and we will become more capable of accepting and responding to change" (p. 79).[12] Cindy Stewart's experience as a leader certainly supports this:

When I became CEO of the Family Health Council of Central Pennsylvania, Inc., in 1999, I needed to shift the culture from a task-oriented hierarchy to a functional, empowered team environment. By leading through questions, I was able to act as a role model and demonstrate my willingness to learn [and] my desire to serve, and that humility can be inspiring. My employees have come to understand that I am a consultative leader and that it is critical to our success that they are knowledgeable of their customer expectations, willingly bring key information to the work process, and seek opportunity for continuous quality improvement. In the past four years, we have increased our budget by $3.5 million . . . opened a new direct service site, and received funding for five new programs. This could not have happened without empowering the staff and unleashing their creativity through questions.

Chad Holliday, former chairman and CEO of DuPont, perhaps sums it up best: "On critical issues, I believe that we must use questions."

This chapter has uncovered the factors that may cause us to have trouble with questions, showing that those factors can be overcome. The testimony from the many leaders supports this point: it can be done. Questions can become an effective management and leadership tool for us when we are comfortable with asking questions, we know what kinds of questions to ask, and we are effective at eliciting full responses to questions and listening to those responses effectively. Those are the topics of the next chapters.

QUESTIONS FOR REFLECTION

1. What are some of the fears I have that cause me not to ask questions?
2. How can I create the time needed to ask questions?
3. How can I develop and improve my questioning skills?
4. How can I develop the courage and confidence to ask questions?
5. Am I willing to ask questions for which I do not already have the answer?
6. Am I afraid of getting an answer that I do not want?
7. How can I become more comfortable as a leader without having all the answers?
8. How can I change a corporate culture that discourages questions?

9. How can I model questioning and reflection in my organization?
10. What are some ways I can help others overcome their fear of asking questions?

Asking the Right Questions

It is important for leaders to fully recognize and understand the power of words. The words we choose to use are metaphors for concepts that define our attitudes and behaviors, structures and concepts. Kouzes and Posner note that "our words evoke images of what we hope to create and how we expect people to behave."[1] The questions that a leader asks send messages about the focus of the organization. They are indeed indicators of what's of most concern to the leader. Our questions are an important measure of how serious we are about our espoused beliefs.

A key for leaders in asking questions is contextual: What do I want my question to accomplish? The questions we employ provide feedback about which values should be attended to and how much energy should be devoted to them. Thus we should be reflecting on what questions we should be asking if we want people to focus on integrity or on trust. Other questions would demonstrate our concern with customer or client satisfaction, or quality, innovation, growth, or personal responsibility.

Questions can be very powerful in focusing attention. When leaders ask questions, they send constituents on mental journeys—quests—in search of answers. These journeys can be positive and productive, inspiring creative problem solving, new insights, and fresh perspective. Unfortunately, our questions can also send people on journeys that are negative and unproductive, provoking defensiveness and self-doubt.

QUESTIONS THAT EMPOWER OR DISEMPOWER

As Chapter 3 notes, one of the reasons that questions cause trouble is that we often ask the wrong questions—that is, questions that disempower others. Questions that disempower focus on the reasons why the person did not or cannot succeed. Such questions result in a defensive or reactive mode, immediately casting the blame on the other person. (Sometimes leaders purposely do this to escape any blame or responsibility themselves.) Poor questions drain energy from the individual and cause reaction rather than creation. Here are some examples of such questions:

- Why are you behind schedule?
- What's the problem with this project?
- Who isn't keeping up?
- Don't you know better than that?

84

We end up creating that which we focus on. By asking disempowering questions, the leader closes the gateway to identifying paths to success. Such questions prevent people from having the opportunity to clarify misunderstandings or achieve goals. *What's wrong?* questions threaten self-esteem and thereby cause people to get mired in their problems. And once in this defensive mode, people are more likely to see themselves as part of the problem rather than as the source of possible solutions.

Empowering questions, on the other hand, get people to think and allow them to discover their own answers, thus developing self-responsibility and transference of ownership for the results. Such questions can help them realize how they are contributing to the whole. Empowering questions build positive attitudes and self-esteem; they remove blocks and open people up to unexpected possibilities while inviting discovery, creativity, and innovation.

Empowering questions help develop alignment within teams and draw out the optimum performance from individual members and the team as a whole. They create a high-energy, high-trust environment and enable people to identify, clarify, and express their wants or needs. Such questions encourage people to take risks, nurture deep relationships, and dissolve resistance to change. Empowering questions enhance your energy level as they focus on what is already working, what can become energizing and supportive, and how best to clarify and achieve common objectives. They also focus on benefits and yield responses that support movement forward toward the objectives.

Jean Halloran, HR manager for Hewlett-Packard, notes that in empowering others, the leader must resist the urge to give people advice. When people ask for help, the leader needs to ask questions so that they come up with their own answers.

So Marilee Goldberg suggests that, instead of asking disempowering questions—such as "Why are you behind schedule?" or "What's the problem with this project?"—leaders ask questions such as these:

- How do you feel about the project thus far?
- What have you accomplished so far that you are most pleased with?
- How would you describe the way you want this project to turn out?
- Which of these objectives do you think will be easiest to accomplish? Which will be most difficult?
- What will be the benefits for our customers if you can meet all these objectives—for our company, for our team, for you personally?
- What key things need to happen to achieve the objective? What kind of support do you need to ensure success?[2]

ROOTS OF GREAT QUESTIONS

Superb questions accomplish a number of wonderful results. So what constitutes a great question for the leader to ask? There is no single correct answer, of course, but most of us who have experience with great questions would agree that they can create the following benefits:

86

- Cause the person to focus and to stretch.
- Create deep reflection.
- Challenge taken-for-granted assumptions that prevent people from acting in new and forceful ways.
- Generate courage and strength.
- Lead to breakthrough thinking.
- Contain the keys that open the door to great solutions.
- Enable people to better view the situation.
- Open doors in the mind and get people to think more deeply.
- Test assumptions and cause individuals to explore why they act in the way that they do as well as why they choose to take action.
- Generate positive and powerful action.

Revans noted that great questions are fresh questions raised in "conditions of ignorance, risk, confusion, or when nobody knows what to do next."[3] Great questions are selfless; they are not asked to illustrate the cleverness of the questioner or to generate information or an interesting response for the questioner. They are generally supportive, insightful, and challenging. They are often unpresumptuous and offered in a sharing spirit.

Great questions are asked at the time when it generates the strongest amount of reflection and learning. Inquisitive leaders make good use of informal meetings, with no script, agenda, or set of action items to discuss. Instead, they start out with empowering questions such as "What's on your mind? Can you tell me about that? Can you help me understand? What should we be worried about?"

Mark Harper, president of wholesale marketing for Cono-coPhillips Petroleum, shared some of his favorite questions with me:

- What is a viable alternative?
- What are the advantages and disadvantages you see in this suggestion?
- Can you more fully describe your concerns?
- What are your goals?
- How would you describe the current reality?
- What are a few options for improvement?
- What will you commit to do by when?

Pam Iorio, former mayor of Tampa, Florida, told me that she identified two great questions that helped her succeed in her difficult and challenging position:

> As I grew in the position as mayor, I saw my role evolve as one who should build leadership in others. I challenge those I work with in an organizational setting to ask this question: "*What have I done to make those around me better, stronger leaders?*" Posing this question places your team in a leadership position, and helps them to understand that their day is not about themselves—it is about growing others. When people see themselves in a supportive, nurturing role, they perform better and take on that mantle of leadership. As they work to build those around them, the entire team is stronger.

The second great question that she often asked was, "Have you forgiven everyone in your life?"

At first people wonder, what in the world does forgiveness have to do with leadership? Well, it really has a lot to do with your effectiveness as a leader. If you are carrying grudges and don't work well with your entire team because of previous slights, altercations, or misunderstandings, you are diminishing your effectiveness as a leader. When you forgive, you are leveraging all of your relationships, working well with your entire team, and maximizing your effectiveness as a leader. I use the example of Nelson Mandela who forgave his captors after twenty-seven years of imprisonment. He said that "forgiveness liberates the soul." Indeed it does, and I ask the question about forgiveness all the time, because it gets people thinking about how forgiveness in their own life will liberate them, lessen their burdens, and help them build stronger relations.

The better the question, the greater the insight gained and the better the solution attained. Tailor your question to the individual you are talking to. Suzanne Milchling, head of the Homeland Defense Business Unit in the Department of Defense, explains how she chooses the questions she asks:

The most valuable questions for me are those that turn individuals to look inward at how they are perceived by others. When I ask some of the employees, "How are you going to do the project?" I get a straight answer. Those I call direct; I can direct them to do something, and they answer my questions in a direct and linear manner.

For other, more abstract thinkers, I need them to cycle within. So I like asking questions like "Would it be useful to get Jim's ideas first? Would he be able to grease the skids for you?" Getting such individuals to recycle their thought patterns in slow motion and out loud to me and others raises questions within them that they may not have thought of before. The abstract thinkers . . . need to be made aware of the details. Their thinking is in patterns, and I want them to understand the "detail" thinkers—the people they may have to convince—the people who think in details and linearly.

Gayle Lantz, president of WorkMatters, suggests the following as great questions for leaders to ask:

- What matters most?
- What is one problem that I can turn into an opportunity?
- What do employees need to hear from me?
- What is our customers' greatest pain?
- What new business relationships will I pursue?
- How will I be more strategic?
- How can I make swift yet smart decisions?
- What leadership skill can—and should—I get better at?
- How will I recognize success?
- What is my biggest fear, and how will I face it?

Often the best, easiest, and most effective way to ask a good question is to simply build on a previous question or on the response to that question. The art and science of carefully listening and then generating an open-ended, creative question will quickly and constructively move individuals toward great insights and effective actions.

TYPES OF EFFECTIVE QUESTIONS

Effective questions are those that accomplish their purpose as well as build a positive relationship between the questioner and questionee. Of course, leaders can ask a variety of types of questions, depending on whether the purpose is to build the individual's or group's capacity to understand and reframe the problem, to build common goals, to develop potential strategies, or to take effective action. Questions should not only build a deeper and better understanding of the problem and possible solutions but also construct better working relations among the problem solvers. Questions can be classified into two general categories: open-ended questions and closed questions. Open-ended questions give the person or group a high degree of freedom in deciding how to respond. In contrast, closed questions seek a short, specific response, like yes or no. Consider the following examples; the topic is the same in both questions, but the responses you get will probably be very different.

- How have sales been going?
- Did you make your sales goal?

Open-Ended Questions

Open-ended questions encourage people to expand ideas and allow exploration of what's important to them or what is comfortable for them to reveal; they also encourage people to do the work of self-reflection and problem solving rather than justifying or defending a position. "I find the open-ended questions most powerful in getting people to respond openly without restricting them to a focus," Effendy Mohamed Rajab told me.

Asking open-ended, unbiased questions also shows respect for the views of others. Open-ended questions invite others to tell their story in their own words. They help to establish rapport, gather information, and increase understanding. When asked properly, they do not lead people toward a specific answer. When asking open-ended questions, one must be ready and willing to listen to the response, which may take a while to unfold and may prompt further questions for clarification.

Open-ended questions should begin with words such as "why" and "how" or phrases such as "What do you think about ... " Open-ended questions can help people think analytically and critically. Ultimately, a good open-ended question should stir discussion and debate. Useful phrases to use with open-ended questions include the following:

- What do you think about . . . ?
- Could you say more about . . . ?
- What possibilities come to mind? What might happen if you . . . ?
- What do you think you will lose if you give up [the point under discussion]?
- What have you tried before?
- What do you want to do next?

Depending on the scope of the question, you may need to coach others through the question by breaking it down into more specific parts. For example, "What do you think of our strategic plan?" is such a broad question that people may grope for a way to begin answering it. You can break it down by homing in on a specific aspect of the strategic plan, such as "What would you identify as the major threats and opportunities we face?"

Why Questions — be careful w/ these

Why questions are perhaps the most important types of open-ended questions for leaders to ask, as these questions force everyone to go into deeper layers of cause and effect, of purposes and assumptions. Such questions are necessary to get under the surface to places where you need to go in order to solve the problem. Although *why* questions may be difficult or uncomfortable for both the leader and the person questioned, they are essential for understanding the deep causes of the situation, and they generate deep learning for the questionee.

Jeff Carew, vice president of collections at Collectcorp, offers this view of the importance of *why* questions:

> What comes out of these discussions is almost always new alternatives that none of us had entered the meeting with. When the staff recognize that I am not going to give "the answer," it is incumbent on them to think. Questions that are most effective are most often ones where there is no clear right or wrong answer, ones that allow us to engage in conversation.

93

An example may be: "I have noticed that volumes have increased dramatically in your area over the last few days; what do you attribute it to?" I will ask the same question again, and if they have only part of the answer, I send them off again until I am satisfied that they have probed all possible reasons. Then we will get together as a group and come up with solutions to the "volume issue."

Remember that *why* questions are really quite natural—we all asked them all the time when we were children. However, they became uncomfortable as we grew up because they caused our authority or expertise or someone else's to be doubted. When asking *why* questions, the leader should watch the tone of voice. The *why* question should indicate curiosity and a search for knowledge, not anger or frustration.

Some *why* questions have such power to make us reflect and perhaps see things in fresh, unpredictable ways that they should be added to our collection of *great questions* to treasure and use often. Questions such as "Why do you think that?" or "Why did this work?" can help the group examine old issues in new, original ways. Here are some other examples of questions with a reliable power to produce rich responses:

- Can that be done in any other way?
- What other options can we think of?
- What resources have we never used?
- What do we expect to happen if we do that?
- What would happen if you did nothing at all?
- What other options do you have?
- What is stopping us?

- What happens if . . . ?
- Have we ever thought of . . . ?

At Toyota, employees are taught to think *why?* consecutively five times. This is a variant of cause-and-effect thinking. If employees think *why?* and find a cause, they try to ask themselves *why?* again. They repeat this five times. Through these five *whys*, they can break down causes to a very specific level. This five-times-why approach is very useful for solving problems.

DuPont Chairman Chad Holliday echoes Toyota's approach. "I believe that one has to ask the *why* question three times to get to the core why," he told me. "*Why* questions have the most power. Most of the time people answer with a surface response to the first *why* question. For example, safety is very important to us, and we believe that most, if not all injuries can be prevented. Someone's finger was cut in a machine. Why? Because the employee put his finger in the machine. Why? Because the machine was not functioning. Why? Because maintenance had not been scheduled."

4, 5, 6
principle

Other Types of Open-Ended Questions

Other types of open-ended questions have a wide variety of uses. Specific types of open-ended questions include the following:

- Explorative questions open up new avenues and insights and lead to new explorations: Have you explored or thought of . . . ? Would such a source help . . . ?

95

- Affective questions invite members to share feelings about an issue: How do you feel about leaving this job?
- Reflective questions encourage more exploration and elaboration: You said there are difficulties with your manager; what do you think causes these difficulties?
- Probing questions invite the person or group to go more deeply into a particular issue, to examine thoroughly or to question closely. This is useful not only for getting more information, but also for getting people to be more open and expansive in their thinking; words such as *describe*, *explain*, *clarify*, *elaborate*, or *expand* get into more depth or breadth on a topic. For example: Can you elaborate on why this is happening?
- Fresh questions challenge basic assumptions: Why must it be that way? What do you always . . . ? Has this ever been tried?
- Questions that create connections establish a systems perspective: What are the consequences of these actions?
- Analytical questions examine causes and not just symptoms: Why has this happened?
- Clarifying questions help free us from ambiguity, but such questions are sometimes difficult to ask. When we hear a question, we tend to think we should know what the other person means, and that it is some fault of ours that we do not understand. Possible questions to ask: What specifically did you mean by that? How exactly would you like that done? Could you explain more about this situation?

People often think of probing questions as a form of attack, but it doesn't need to be that way. "I ask probing questions because my people want to look good and I want them to look good," Suzanne Milchling told me. "The goal is to get them to learn on their own." When I asked how probing questions help people to look good, she replied, "It is the question that was unanticipated and *not* asked that gets our people in trouble."

Working with Open-Ended Questions

Open-ended questions can address either content or process issues, and content and process questions have different roles. Spitzer and Evans (1997) distinguish them as follows: content questions ask about the data used to solve a problem or make a decision; process questions focus on *how* the problem was solved or the decision made. Both are essential to good problem solving and decision making.

Most leaders focus on content questions, which come more naturally; process questions, on the other hand, require conscious attention. Starting with the appropriate process questions gives people access to insights that help them formulate and explain their thinking. In comparison, starting with content questions risks leading people and limiting the range of their responses. Thus the preferred sequence is to start with process questions and then proceed to content questions.

Some leaders are uncomfortable asking open-ended questions, because by definition they allow the respondent to take the conversation to new places. In other words, open-ended questions give a large measure of control to the person who answers. Leaders who like to maintain control tend to focus on closed questions, which call for only a brief response and

97

allow the questioner to decide what to say or ask next. Asking closed questions can become a habit. But as we learn to ask open-ended questions, the people in the organization benefit, as they think through their responses to express what they want to say. And with their answers, we find out more about what they think and feel from their perspective.

Ask lots of open-ended questions. Open-ended questions that begin with *why* or *how* get people thinking and talking. You may be surprised at how much talk you unleash. You may learn a lot, and even if you just listen, they'll walk away happy and feeling heard and respected.

Closed Questions

Closed questions call for a specific answer—either yes or no—or call for the respondent to select an answer from a limited range of choices. Closed questions often begin with *what, when,* or *how many,* or ask the respondent to agree or disagree with a statement. Here are some examples of closed questions:

- How many people will be affected?
- Did you agree with this decision?
- When should we meet?
- What time is it?
- Do you prefer Plan A or Plan B?

As noted, open-ended questions tend to explore possibilities, feelings, and reasons why. In contrast, closed questions tend to focus on facts: what, when, where. Because they call for specific responses, closed questions also tend to be quick and easy to answer.

Closed questions are useful at the beginning and end of conversations. As you start a conversation, asking a simple closed question makes it easy for people to answer and doesn't force them to reveal too much about themselves. For example, you might begin a conversation by asking, "Is this a good time for us to talk?" At the end of a conversation, closed questions can help you clarify or seek further understanding of the results of the discussion and reach closure on a decision or course of action. Salespeople often use closed questions when they move in to close the sale: "If I can deliver this tomorrow, will you sign for it now?"

If you are not clear about what another person is saying, a direct closed question can quickly clarify the situation. Open-ended questions, as discussed earlier, can also be used for clarification, but closed questions are often more direct: "It sounds like you're saying that we need to speed up action on this. Is that right?" or "Do you want me to take you off the project?" Such questions help bring exploratory discussions launched by open-ended questions down to earth, remove vagueness and ambiguity, and help move the group forward.

Of course, all these questions can be followed up with additional questions. Follow-up questions are usually even more powerful, as they enable you to acquire a deeper understanding of the situation, demonstrate that you were listening, and enable you to achieve double- and triple-loop levels of learning.

UNHELPFUL QUESTIONS

In addition to disempowering questions, two other types of questions that are not helpful from the leader are leading questions—those that force or encourage the person or group to respond in the way intended by the questioner ("You wanted to do it by yourself, didn't you?")—and multiple questions; that is, a string of questions put together to meet the needs of the questioner but confusing to the responder.

Leading questions either include the answer within the question ("Don't you agree that John is the problem here?"), come with extra baggage that suggests the expected answer ("What do you think about John? I don't think he's a team player . . ."), or include some form of carrot or stick to prod the other person to produce the expected answer ("Everyone else on the team thinks John is the problem. What about you?").

The problem with leading questions is that they are not genuine attempts to seek information; they are not-so-subtle efforts to influence, persuade, or coerce agreement. They are not questions at all. When there is a power discrepancy between the questioner and the respondent, leading questions can cause alienation and disempowerment. Even when no power imbalance is involved, leading questions can fray relationships.

Multiple questions, especially if they are closed questions, can result in the person who's being subjected to them feeling interrogated. It is tempting—and often accurate—for the respondent to feel that the questioner has a private agenda with no concern for anyone else's well-being or opinions.

FINDING GREAT QUESTIONS

Albert Einstein was perhaps one of the greatest questioners of all time as well as a great scientist. As he once observed, "The most important thing is not to stop questioning. Curiosity has its own reason for existing."[4] Einstein recognized the importance of asking questions; he once stated that if he had an hour of time to work on a problem, he would spend the first fifty-nine minutes coming up with a great question. His question about the relationship between mass, speed, and energy, which led to the formula $E = mc^2$, is surely one of history's greatest questions.

In addition to being a physicist, Einstein was also a gifted violinist, and he enjoyed teaching children how to play the violin. On one occasion, his professorial colleagues asked Einstein why he "wasted" so much time teaching children how to play the violin when he could better use that time working in his laboratory. Einstein responded: "It is not a waste of time. The reason why I love teaching children is because they ask such great questions!" And Einstein often remarked that he was able to ask fresh questions because he could still ask like a child.

We all need to find ways to ask great questions and to recognize that the search for great questions is never completed. Peter Senge offers these suggestions as to where to search for great questions:

- *Assessing the landscape*: Get a feel for the larger context; scan the horizon as well as the contours of the current business landscape; notice indicators that point to storms as well as sunny skies.
- *Discovering core questions*: Look for patterns for questions, cluster the questions, and consider the relationships that

appear among them; notice what pops up in order to uncover the deeper themes that the initial questions reveal.

- *Creating images of possibilities*: Imagine what the situation would be if big questions were answered; create vivid images of possibilities.

- *Evolving workable strategies*: Workable strategies begin to emerge in response to compelling questions and to the images of possibility that these questions evoke.[5]

Throughout the pages of this book, you will see numerous examples of types of great questions asked by leaders for various purposes. In the next chapter, I turn to the most effective ways to ask these questions.

QUESTIONS FOR REFLECTION

1. How can I ask great questions?
2. How can I create images of possibilities?
3. Do I know what I wish to accomplish with my questions?
4. What are empowering questions that I could ask?
5. How can I change my disempowering questions to more positive questions?
6. How can I ask more open-ended questions?
7. Which types of open-ended questions do I tend to use more or less frequently?
8. How can I ask questions that enable me to learn what is most important to the other person?
9. When would it be best for me to use closed questions?
10. What questions can I use to help those around me become more successful?

The Art of Asking Questions

Grasping the art of questioning can lead to impressive results; asking inappropriate questions usually closes off learning. But even when we work hard to make sure the questions we ask are appropriate, we can undermine the process by asking questions carelessly. The attitude, mindset, pace, timing, environment, and context all can affect the impact of our questions. Asking a question at the right time in the right manner with the right person is just as important as the content of the question itself. Good questions can become great questions when the science of inquiring is blended with the art of questioning.

JUDGER VERSUS LEARNER: THE MINDSET FOR ASKING QUESTIONS

As Adams emphasizes, our mindset frames how we see the world.[1] It simultaneously programs what we believe to be our personal limitations and what we see as our possibilities.

Mindsets define the parameters of our actions and interactions and affect, either explicitly or implicitly, outcomes in any area of focus. They are a determinant in the types of questions we ask ourselves and others. In addition, our individual mindset determines how we observe, understand, and accept ourselves and others.

Adams refers to two types of mindsets that may reside in the questioner: learner and judger. In the *learner* mindset, the questioner seeks to be responsive to life's circumstances. When we are focused on learning, we seek to understand the past as a way of guiding our actions in the future. Leaders with the learner mindset tend to be optimistic and to presuppose new possibilities, a hopeful future, and sufficient resources. They exude optimism, possibilities, and hope.

The *judger* mindset, on the other hand, is reactive. Leaders with the judger mindset tend to focus on the past, not as a means of learning but to apportion praise or, more likely, blame. When our focus is on judging, we worry more about fixing responsibility for problems than on working with others to find solutions. Judging questions result in win-lose encounters, as they all too often operate in an attack-or-defend paradigm. Leaders with the judger mentality tend to believe they know the answers already anyway.

Leaders who focus on learning rather than judging can be flexible and relate to others in a win-win manner that facilitates the search for creative solutions. Such leaders establish and nurture relationships that operate collaboratively and innovatively. A leader with the learner mindset can be more

104

open to new possibilities than one who prefers to judge, and less attached to personal opinions and the need to be right.

"It is important to be benign when asking questions," says Michael Coleman, president of Alcoa's Rigid Packaging business unit in Knoxville, Tennessee. "Seek the cause without being accusatory. I firmly believe that the strength of questions is a tried-and-true way to find root causes. I take care in how I ask questions. I do not demonstrate with my body language that my mind is made up, that a person is being attacked or getting sabotaged. If I act in this way, I do not get the full or complete answer; the person worries more about getting into trouble and being foolish than about listening to, and responding to my questions."

According to Adams, the learner mindset exemplified by Michael Coleman leads to much greater effectiveness, breakthroughs, and transformations. Although it may sometimes be more difficult and challenging to operate with a learner mindset, it is much more rewarding for everyone involved. A learner mindset leads to thinking objectively, creating solutions, and relating in a win-win way. Leaders with a learner mindset ask genuine questions; that is, questions to which they don't already know the answers. Consider another comment by Michael Coleman: "I believe that leaders often misuse questions. I use questions to gain knowledge or to teach. I don't ask questions that I already know the answers to or to embarrass someone—this sabotages the whole purpose of questions."

A leader who is habitually judgmental, on the other hand, puts employees on the defensive because they live in constant fear of being judged and found wanting. A judging attitude causes employees to hide their mistakes, defend their behavior, and refuse to ask for help or admit their weaknesses or vulnerabilities. This can lead to a downward spiral .

Exhibit 5.1 summarizes these two divergent mindsets as well as the divergent relationships that result, which in turn result in totally different questions and questioning styles on the part of the leader.

Exhibit 5.1. Learner or Judger Mindsets and Relationships

Mindsets	
Judger	**Learner**
Judgmental (of self and others)	Accepting (of self and others)
Reactive and automatic	Responsive and thoughtful
Knows it all already	Values not knowing
Places blame	Accepts responsibility
Inflexible and rigid	Flexible and adaptive
Either/or thinking	Both/and thinking
Self-righteous	Inquisitive
Has only personal perspective	Considers perspectives of others
Defends assumptions	Questions assumptions
Expresses more statements and opinions	Offers more questions and curiosity
Sees possibilities as limited	Sees possibilities as unlimited
Primary mood: protective	Primary mood: curiosity

We all have both mindsets, and we have the power to choose where we operate from in any moment.

Relationships	
Judger	**Learner**
Win-lose relationships	Win-win relationships
Sense of being separate	Sense of being connected
Fears differences	Values differences
Debates	Dialogues
Criticizes	Critiques
Listens for:	Listens for:
• Right/wrong	• Facts
• Agreement/disagreement	• Understanding
• Differences	• Commonalities
Feedback perceived as rejection	Feedback perceived as worthwhile
Seeks to attack or defend	Seeks to resolve and create

We all relate from both mindsets, and we have the power to choose how we relate in any moment.

Source: Adapted from Adams, 2012.

Here are some examples of questions asked from the learner mindset, according to Adams:

- What's good or useful about this?
- What possibilities does this open up?
- What can we do about this?

- How can we stay on track?
- What can we learn from this?

For contrast, here are some examples of judging questions:

- Why is this a failure?
- What's wrong with you?
- Whose fault is it?
- Why can't you get it right?

By consciously adopting a learning mindset, we can become more open to new possibilities and ask questions more effectively. When those around us sense that we do have a learning attitude, that we are eager for new information and new insights, they become more open and thoughtful in answering our questions. The flow of information and ideas opens up, and problem solving, teamwork, and innovation is enhanced.

ADOPTING A LEARNER MINDSET

It can be difficult, in a high-pressure business environment, to get away from a judger mindset. After all, managers are responsible for results; they must make sure that people are held accountable. When the results don't measure up, when things go wrong, the manager has to find out what happened and why. But there is an important distinction: finding out *what* happened and *why* does not mean finding out *who*. Indeed, effective leaders know that the question of *who* often must be left off the table to get accurate answers to the questions of *what* and *why*. Even when issues of *who* must be addressed, effective leaders know that the best approach is to be the supportive coach rather than the judging boss.

Coaching is the opposite of bossing. A coaching-type relationship helps people work out issues and find their own answers through the skillful use of probing questions. A supportive attitude of mutual discovery on the part of the leader creates trust and builds support in return. Coaches help employees recognize their strengths and uncover their blind spots; they can offer additional possibilities and options that employees had not considered in evaluating their situations. Such leaders listen carefully and thoroughly, especially when they don't like or agree with what they are hearing, and they are willing to suspend their own opinions in the face of new data.

Such leaders possess a set of attitudes and dispositions that encourage them to want to ask useful questions and to ask them in a fair-minded way. They are not concerned with who is right; whoever finds the better conclusion first is not relevant; what matters is the search for better conclusions. If you give signals to those around you that you are their partner in a discovery process intended to enrich you both, they will see your critical questions as a tool that is indispensable to both of you.

Sue Whitt, global head of Abbott Labs' Pharmaceutical Regulatory Operations, explained to me how she used questions to help take the edge off being the boss and develop a coaching relationship with her staff:

> Through the use of questions, I could mitigate some of the negative that comes with positional power. I got a lot of

energy from my staff as questions helped them forget that I had this authority. Questions actually led to a dialogue. When projects were off track, I asked them to think of why they made that choice. This got them thinking and speaking. I would ask, "Why did you take this path? How does this connect to the goals set?" By asking *why* and *what* questions (simple but effective), less often than *who* and *when* questions, I was much more effective at [helping them navigate] the system. I could give them some of the who and when; but not the what and the why.

Here are some specific suggestions that can help you coach others and adopt a learning attitude:

- Respond without judging the thoughts, feelings, or situations of other people.
- Consider yourself a beginner, regardless of experience.
- Avoid focusing on your own role (which can lead to a self-protective approach) and take the role of an outside observer, researcher, or reporter.
- Look at the situation from multiple perspectives, especially your respondents'.
- Look for win-win solutions.
- Be tolerant of yourself and of others.
- Ask clarifying questions.
- Accept change as constant, and embrace it.

HOW TO FRAME QUESTIONS

Framing questions involves much more than choosing the right words to express them. Questions are framed by the entire context that surrounds them. Indeed, the most important part of framing questions has already been discussed: asking questions as a part of a learning process rather than a judging exercise. By making it clear that our questions are attempts to learn, we have already gone a long way toward framing them in a way that will yield positive results. Conversely, if our attitude is critical and judgmental, no preamble and no amount of wordsmithing will overcome the larger message our attitude sends. David Smyk of Healthcare Executive Partners says, "The proper framing of questions allows one to view the questioner as a team member who can assist in achieving a successful outcome and not as an obstacle to the process."

Even if we have a sincere desire to learn, old habits die hard. As leaders, we need to question our questions. It is very easy, when questioning, to let our own values, preferences, and biases leak into what we are asking. We must develop the attitudes and skills to notice, analyze, and revise our questions. Before we ask a question, we should preview it in our minds from the other person's point of view to determine whether the question as phrased will be truly helpful. If you are unsure how a question might be taken, be frank and say so. For example, you might say, "I'm not sure how to ask this question, but . . . ?" This is a way of defusing any issue that might arise from the way you ask a difficult question.

Given the realities of organizational life and positional power, it is often helpful to bend over backward to be clear that you are not seeking a scapegoat. For example, if there has been an accident, rather than come right out and ask "How did it happen?" you might preface your question with a statement like this: "It's important that we analyze every accident to see what factors contributed to it so that we can prevent similar accidents in the future." Once the framework for the question is established—that it is about the future, and focuses on prevention (not about the past, and not about blame or responsibility)—then you can ask, "How did it happen?" When you frame the question in this way, the answers you get are likely to be open and informative.

In today's diverse workplace, we need to pay particular attention to how we frame our questions.

Effendy Mohamed Rajab of the World Organization of the Scout Movement in Geneva observes, "Questions, in many cultures, can be threatening if done improperly. Many people are not comfortable when being asked 'why' a number of times, especially in the presence of someone who is their senior. Therefore it is important that you create a positive climate for the dialogue and observe the body language."

In the same vein, Isabel Rimanoczy (an executive coach and a partner with Leadership in International Management) told me, "In Thailand, questions can be seen as challenging the opinion of another person, and rule number one is that no one should 'lose face.' My experience led me to reframe the question as a gift for someone, as a sign of interest and curiosity. This reframing totally changed the perception of the question, and the group easily adopted the questioning process." Framing questions as a demonstration of interest in another person's point of view is helpful in building relationships. Similarly, it can also be useful to frame a question as a request for a favor: "I value your opinion highly, so I would appreciate it if you could tell me . . ." In this way, you are asking for a gift rather than demanding something in a manner the other person may regard as improper or threatening.

It is best if the leader frames questions in a positive way, using what Cooperrider refers to as *"appreciative inquiry."*[2] Appreciative inquiry is "the study and exploration of what gives life to human systems when they function at their best."[3] This approach to personal and organizational change is based on the assumption that questions and dialogue about strengths, successes, values, hopes, and dreams are themselves transformational (for both the questioner and the person questioned). It is a relational process of inquiry, grounded in affirmation and appreciation.

So instead of asking what went wrong, the wise leader will tend to ask questions that focus on what has gone well, what could be done, how the situation could be improved. The approach will guide the group in seeking what might be, rather than what is not. The focus remains on improvement and continuous learning rather than on complaining and venting. By being open-minded and not negative, the leader encourages fresher and broader ranges of responses.

Mike Stice, CEO of Access Midstream Partner, told me that he frames his questions primarily as a way to help his team understand why the organization is now in its current status, whether that is positive or negative. He says, "Asking questions about a positive outcome can help us to determine the potential to replicate the event in other situations and thereby capture further rewards. The inquiry into the negative outcomes is to identify the specific circumstances to be avoided to ensure that these negative results are not repeated."

TIMING FOR QUESTIONS

Finding the ideal time for asking questions is an art. If we bring up questions too early in a process, the group or individual may lack the experience to have sufficient data to respond adequately, and thus we may miss an opportunity for understanding. If the questions come too late, we may miss an opportunity for learning and frustrate the participants in the group, who have been struggling without help and support for too long. Experience will make the leader grow more comfortable and confident in timing questions for optimal results.

STEPS IN THE QUESTIONING PROCESS

Asking questions can be and often is a very simple process. Questions often just pop up in the course of a conversation; they get answered, and the conversation moves on. When, however, you find that you are confronting a difficult issue, and you want to plan things out ahead of time, it can be useful to follow a simple process. First, break the ice and get the conversation going. Second, set the stage for the conversation by explaining what you want to talk about. Third, ask what you want to ask. Fourth, listen attentively to the answers. Fifth, and most important, follow up.

Breaking the Ice

It is useful to start with casual questions to put people at ease and get them talking. As noted in Chapter 4, a simple closed question ("Is this a good time to talk?") can often get the ball rolling. Friendly, open-ended questions ("How's your day been?") can be used to encourage the other person to open up. Keep the tone friendly as you move to set the stage for your question.

Setting the Stage

As you set the stage, you are framing the question by establishing the context and background for the conversation. Setting the stage is primarily about you, not the other person. As noted, a learner mindset, not a judger mindset, is critical to getting free and honest answers and open conversation.

Be forthright in saying that the purpose of the conversation is to learn, not to judge. It is often helpful to open up yourself and offer some self-disclosure. You might say something like, "I have been concerned that our sales are not as strong as we hoped" or "I am really excited by this new program we are trying out." The point is to let the other person know where you are coming from. If you are concerned about a problem, describe the problem as you see it, as objectively as possible—and let the other person respond to your description before moving ahead. If you are looking for new ideas, say so.

One way to set the stage is to explain what you hope the outcome of the conversation will be. Spell it out, as in the following statements:

- I hope to get a better understanding of why we are having this problem.
- I want a better feel for how customers are responding to our new products.
- I want to understand how you feel about my plan for the unit.

As long as your objective is learning rather than judging, specifying your objective clearly should not be threatening to the other person.

The key to framing good questions, according to Kouzes and Posner, is to think about the "quest" in your questions.[4] What do you want this person to think about? What do you want to learn? A questing mindset shows that you care about the other person. There's a popular saying about this: people don't care how much you know until they know how much you care.

The leader should not enter the questing situation with a sole focus on help and advice, as this attitude can evoke defiance, dependency, and defensiveness—all undesirable responses. Asking about how to make things happen instead of focusing on why they don't work is the type of questing that a leader should pursue.

In his classic *Questioning and Teaching*, Dillon writes that questioning our purpose can be answered by discovering our intent with respect to answers. "Why do I need this information? What is it that I want to know or find out? What will I do with the answer? How will the answer work to tell or show me what I intend it to do?"[5]

Once the purpose of the conversation is clear, you should move directly to asking your questions.

Asking Your Questions

Make sure your questions are empowering rather than disempowering, as discussed in Chapter 4. Open-ended questions are much more likely to generate a positive, nondefensive response than are closed questions, which allow for only a limited range of possible responses. Leading questions will be seen for what they are: attempts at manipulation. "An effective question must be an inquiry," Cindy Stewart of Family Health Council of Central Pennsylvania says. "Too often I have seen people try to embed their solution in their question." She cautions that maneuvering people into accepting a solution is not usually effective. "When dealing with difficult work problems, the more ownership employees have in the solution, the more successful the resolution," she notes. These are some of the questions Stewart has found to be most effective:

- How does your solution meet your goals and objectives?
- What are you trying to accomplish?
- What will your customer expect?
- How does this advance our strategic goals?
- How is this supported by our core values?
- What are the factors you considered in reaching this solution?

When asking questions, keep your focus on the questioner and the question, not on the million other concerns you may have. You can't listen and at the same time think of the next thing that you are going to ask or say. The quality of the response is affected not only by the content of the question but also by its manner of delivery, especially its pace and timing. Try to maintain a steady pace. Do not let your eye contact waver. The key to this skill is that you must be genuinely curious and not make the employee feel judged, interrogated, or manipulated. Use verbal encouragers such as "I didn't know that; tell me more. What else happened?"

Questioning leaders are curious. Leaders ask better questions when they are curious rather than demanding. Einstein observed: "The important thing is not to stop questioning. Curiosity has its own reason for existing." Seldom do we search or explore for what we already know with certainty. We ask questions about areas unfamiliar to us. The act of inquiry requires sincere curiosity and openness to new possibilities, new directions, and new understandings. As John Wooden, the legendary and highly successful basketball coach, notes, "It's what you learn after you know everything that counts."

It is not necessary to shout or use high volume when asking questions. Often the more softly the question is asked, the more powerful it is—unlike statements, which may be more effective and have greater impact when they are made loudly and emphatically. The manner of introducing questions should be gentle and not arrogant.

Try to ask one question at a time. Too often we overwhelm or confuse people by asking several questions simultaneously. Allow for a response before asking the next question. Many of us tend to ask questions one after another to maintain control of the floor, or because we may not be sure whether and when we may get the next opportunity to ask a question, or because we have not thought through the question, or because we want to control or manipulate the response to the first question. Such a questioning approach leads to responses of poor quality. People may resist multiple questions, feeling they are at an interrogation. Inexperienced or impatient questioners ask flurries of questions that reveal more of a desire for control than a search for the truth.

Remember that you are engaging in a conversation, not an interrogation, and you should be prepared to be questioned in turn as the conversation moves along. Listen to how you are talking as well as to the answers you get. If you find yourself talking quickly or getting shorter and shorter answers, back off for a time or otherwise slow down the proceedings. Also, you as the leader should be comfortable in reflecting and taking your time in responding to a good or great question that you have been asked. Focus on what is being said so that you fully understand the intent of the question. Pay attention to the words spoken as well as the implied content and meaning embedded in both the content and the manner of the response. It is important to suspend your own preconceptions, associations, and judgments. And be careful not to begin planning your next question. This often requires allowing "wait time" before responding so as to be sure that the other person has really finished.

Leaders should be careful not to rush the responses to their questions. A good question will often cause the recipient to step back and reflect. A great question will cause even more reflection and silence. Leaders should be comfortable when there is no immediate response to a question. Allow the people being questioned to reflect, and let them know that you are comfortable with the silence. Silence tells others that you expect them to respond and to continue. Providing time and silence allows

119

others to dig deeper into their thought processes to answer the question.[6]

Effective questioners understand that not all questions need to be answered immediately. Give people time to mull over your request for information and develop some ideas. The question will continue to incubate in their minds, and perhaps when that same question is asked later, a wealth of responses will emerge. Putting others under a tight deadline inhibits open-minded thinking. Time permitting, it's better to say, "Let's get together in a few days and bounce this around. In the meantime, give it some thought. I would like to have a few suggestions to check out." As David Rock, president of NeuroLeadership, told me, questions are most effective when there is not a rush or push for immediate responses. Allowing the brain to relax and reflect is necessary so there is a sense of reward rather than threat in the mind. Sometimes there is more power and value in the question and the reflection that it causes than in the responses that it generates.

If you actually meet resistance, the best response is to stay quiet. You have to give a person time to think. The person has to process thoughts and feelings about why you are now asking questions and then go through the process of formulating the answer. We sometimes forget or find it difficult to look at the world from a perspective other than our own.

Listening and Showing Interest in the Response

When you get a response, say "thank you." This will increase the likelihood that you'll get more and deeper answers the next time you ask. When your questioning respects people's thought processes, you support their own questioning of long-held assumptions. It is much harder to ask skillful questions than to give advice. And for many years managers have received positive feedback for having the answers and giving advice. But *our* answers work for *us*. We often need to let others find answers that work best for *them*.

If you are sincerely taking a learning attitude in asking questions, you should not shift into a judgmental mode once you have gotten an answer. Judging or criticizing responses to your questions will only close off learning and innovation. Says Jeff Carew of Collectcorp:

> During my staff meetings I bring up agenda items pertaining to the group's area of responsibility. We may have a customer with a dramatic increase in unexpected volume that requires immediate attention. I will start by asking them to clearly define the problem; then we start listing alternatives to fix our problem. I keep prodding them to give more alternatives and will only volunteer some of my alternatives after I have exhausted all of their alternatives. All of them understand that no alternative is wrong or inappropriate, that we want to get everything out on the table. After the options are out, we then look at the up and down side of each and continue to proceed to narrow them down until we have a basic course of action. This is the way we solve the problems of the day, week, or month.

Peter Drucker and others have noted that the most important thing in communication is to hear what isn't being said.

This obviously requires careful, good listening. Effective listening skills are critical if you wish to get the most out of questions. It is a wonderful gift to have people give you their full attention. It can also be helpful to have people reflect back to you what they heard and felt while listening to you. We sometimes are unaware of our anger or pain about a situation because we have buried the feelings. When the feelings are noticed and reflected back, we have a greater awareness of ourselves.

By fully listening to employees without interrupting or leaping in to solve their problems, you set the stage that allows them to find their own answers. Your interruptions, no matter how well intentioned, take the floor away from an employee and put the focus back on you. When you are certain that the employee has completed a thought, then reflect back what you heard and observed.

The executive director for organization development at Novartis, Robert Hoffman, explains why he thinks listening is so important:

> I am reminded of [Stephen R.] Covey's habit number 5: Seek first to understand, then to be understood. It is important that I listen empathically and try getting inside the other person's frame of reference so I can listen with one purpose: understanding. One cannot truly understand the other person's position without questions. I then work on ensuring, also through questions, that I have clearly communicated my thoughts and ideas.

My staff is most appreciative that I give them the chance to participate as a full equal. I show this by the way I listen to them and trust their judgment. People really appreciate being asked a question and then action being taken as a result of that question.

According to Frances Hesselbein, "We need leaders who practice the art of listening, practice Peter Drucker's 'think first, speak last.' Leaders who are healers and unifiers use listening to include, not exclude—building consensus, appreciating differences, finding common concepts, common language, common ground."[7]

As a leader, you have a number of ways to demonstrate that you are listening to and caring about the person you are questioning:

- Pause at the end of a question so that the answerer can think, formulate, and deliver an answer.
- Once you have asked your questions, listen.
- Use steady eye contact and supportive nods; be alert for "iceberg tips"—body language, facial expressions, gestures, and vague comments that hint a willingness to contribute more information or opinions if encouraged. Staying silent is more than just not talking. It means keeping eye contact, staying still, and feeling comfortable while you wait.
- Be certain to demonstrate that you really want to grasp what is being said. Ask questions that indicate your willingness to encounter and accept new conclusions. Many times it is necessary to ask clarifying questions so as to assure yourself that you have a complete understanding of the situation.

- Listen patiently, without interrupting. Interrupting may show you are not interested in the response or the respondent.
- Use reflective listening, hearing the words and reading the emotional content.
- Restate what you heard in your own words and ask whether your understanding of the argument is consistent with what was said.
- Voice your critical questions as if you are curious. Nothing is more deadly to the effective use of critical thinking than an attitude of "Aha, I caught you making an error."
- Request additional reasons that might enable the person to make a stronger argument than the one originally provided.
- Ask the other person for permission to allow you to explore any weaknesses in the reasoning. The idea with this strategy is to encourage the other person to examine the argument with you.
- Convey the impression that you and the other person are collaborators, working toward the same objective—improved knowledge and results.
- Show respect for their views by asking open-ended, unbiased questions.
- Focus your listening by asking questions such as "What is useful about this?" and "What can I learn?" rather than "Whose fault is this?"
- Help people learn through the process of answering.

Leaders need to be careful not to interrupt; rather than jumping in, they should first make sure they have a complete understanding of the situation. Careful observation and good note taking allow them to be in tune with who is saying what, how, when, and to whom. Active listening requires a great deal of attention. This strong listening enables us to acquire a wider and more holistic view.

Leaders must have a deep commitment to listening intently to others and thereby become better able to identify and clarify the will of a group. To be an effective questioner, wait for the answer—don't provide it yourself. An insatiable, nonjudgmental curiosity will enable a leader to ask the many great questions needed by individuals, groups, and organizations.

Following Up

Following up after a questioning conversation is critically important. Someone who has openly and thoughtfully answered your questions deserves to know what you did with the information. Likewise, someone who honestly responds to a question by expressing dissatisfaction with a process or concerns about a direction will feel ignored if the concerns are never mentioned again. Leaders who do not follow up after posing questions will soon find themselves in difficulties. Cindy Stewart says,

> One important thing I have learned, and try to impart to my executive team, is that a leader who relies on questions alone will ultimately be viewed as insincere and not trustworthy. The power of questions can only be realized through learning, follow-up, and change. The leader who asks questions

and doesn't pay attention to the answers quickly loses credibility. My use of questions comes from a true desire to learn from my employees. That is reinforced by my efforts to follow up on their answers, which will result in visible changes in process, procedure, or operations.

Executive coach Marshall Goldsmith writes that for leaders, "asking and learning will have to be more than an academic exercise. The process will have to produce meaningful, positive change. By learning how to follow up efficiently and effectively in an extremely busy world, leaders will enable key stakeholders to see the positive actions that result from the input they were requested to provide."[8] When we don't follow up on the responses we get to our questions, others will see our questions as an academic exercise, or worse—as Cindy Stewart says, they will see us as insincere and untrustworthy.

Alcoa's Mike Coleman agrees that following up—or, as he puts it, "giving something in return"—is critical. He says, "It is important that I give them something in return after I have digested their responses to my question. I need to give them information and action, to show the benefit of their responses."

SINCERE LISTENING AND LEARNING

Although this chapter has presented a lot of strategies and techniques for asking questions effectively, the art of questioning is really not about tips and techniques at all. It all comes down to being sincere in wanting to learn rather than blame, in wanting to listen to responses openly and nonjudgmentally, and in following up on the conversation with action. When we are sincere in these ways, the conversation flows almost effortlessly.

QUESTIONS FOR REFLECTION

1. Do I understand the differences between judging questions and learning questions?
2. How do I build a mindset of learning when I ask questions?
3. What questions can I use to demonstrate a learning mindset?
4. What are some ways for me to better frame my questions?
5. How do I determine when is the best time to ask questions?
6. How can I seek the cause without being accusatory?
7. What are some ways I can set the stage when asking questions?
8. How can I better show interest in the responses to my questions?
9. Do I make an effort to carefully listen so I can ask better questions?
10. How can I be more effective with my follow-up questions?

Creating a Questioning Culture

The goal for the inquiring leader is to change the corporate culture from one of telling to one of asking; to help everyone see and understand that questions need to become their primary communications tool. As noted in Chapter 2, changing the culture of an organization pays dividends. And there is no more effective way of creating a questioning culture than by using questions to do so. "Questions have had the impact of changing the culture from one of employees' feeling disenfranchised to one of ownership," Mark Thornhill told me. As CEO of the Midwest Region of the American Red Cross, Thornhill has adopted a questioning style of leadership. "It has empowered [my team] and caused significant change in attitudes and productivity. It has enabled my manager [and me] to better understand each other."

THE LEADER'S ROLE IN SHAPING A QUESTIONING CULTURE

How can a leader develop a questioning culture? Here are some strategies that can build a powerful learning and questioning culture:

- Start at the top. The questioning culture must begin with the most senior leaders, who model the frequent use of good questions.
- Create an environment that enables people to challenge the status quo, take risks, and ask more questions. Recognize that many standard practices, policies, and procedures are no longer valuable to the company—if they ever were.
- Connect the values and processes of the organization to the use of questions.
- Optimize the opportunities to ask questions by building questioning into every business activity, including formal and informal meetings, sales calls, conferences with clients, or presentations.
- Reward and appreciate questioners; promote risk taking and tolerate mistakes.
- Provide training for people to be better at and more comfortable with asking questions.

Each of these strategies reinforces behavior connected to the six hallmarks of a questioning culture.

Leaders Model the Way

A number of successful leaders have modeled the way to effectively use questions. August Busch III, when chairman

130

and CEO of Anheuser-Busch, encouraged openness in his nine-member board. He insisted that each member come prepared to present an opinion and back it up. When tough issues emerged, he asked executives with opposite points of view to present their perspectives. August Busch attributed much of the success of his company to the questioning and learning culture he developed at Anheuser-Busch.[1]

Charles Heimbold, former chairman and CEO of Bristol-Myers Squibb, describes how he built his company into a learning organization. He and other top managers were committed to asking questions—they did not dictate. Effective leaders at BMS, he notes, "know that a good question is much more powerful than an order. They are less likely to tell someone the right answer and more likely to suggest who might have expertise, or who might be available internally or externally for the person to talk with in order to bring the best information to bear on the work."[2] BMS leaders were constantly walking around asking questions and "looking under rocks." They searched for opinions and ideas extensively inside and outside of the organization. Senior managers were expected to travel and cover a wide range of competitors, suppliers, customers, academics, and other labs so as to get new information and opinions. Leaders encouraged their people to do the same by inviting them to accompany them as well as to go out on their own. Bristol-Myers Squibb became a vital and stimulating organization, with the kind of energy and electricity that marks a culture that supports innovation.

Chad Holliday, president and CEO of DuPont, is another leader who models the way in his use of questions. In fact, he says, "As I have moved up during my thirty-five years here at DuPont, I have used questions more and more." Early in his career, he says, he was trained "in the nature of questions, and . . . how to ask good questions." He adds, "I tend to ask questions to find out from others how to shape solutions, how to get alignment more quickly." He continues:

> Inside DuPont, we have a common and clear objective, so the questioning process works well. When our senior people come together, we have a framework that guides our discussions. It requires self-discipline to keep questioning; there is a great temptation to make statements, especially when you are in a hurry and want to do things quickly.
>
> On critical issues, I believe that we must use questions. At our meetings, we begin by identifying the three critical questions that we need to answer during that meeting. At the end, we ask how well we did. The leader of the meeting determines the questions. Every meeting has a purpose and should have some final products; usually the products are the answers to those questions.

Successful and effective leaders continually search for opportunities to ask questions. When the Center for Creative Leadership studied 191 successful executives, they discovered that the key to their success was creating opportunities to ask, and then asking questions.[3]

Leaders model the way not only by asking questions but also by demonstrating their willingness to learn and change. Edgar Schein notes that leaders must have extraordinary levels of motivation and self-confidence to enable them to go through the inevitable pain of learning and change.[4] They must also have the emotional strength to manage their own and others' anxiety as learning and change become more and more a way of life. Margaret Wheatley points out that leaders should be champions of thinking, reflecting, and open-ended spaces.[5] They must recognize that their colleagues cannot become smarter by action alone. Great leaders are eager to see people learn. They understand and appreciate how adults learn, and they see learning as a way of life.

Questioning leaders can become great teachers and colearners. Leaders should look for creative ways to find teaching and learning opportunities. Through questions, they turn every interaction with their people into a potential learning event. They often set aside time to teach leadership outside of scheduled activities. Practicing action learning, taking risks, seeking innovative answers, and asking fresh questions all exhibit a leader's solid learning practices and skills to employees. Institutions that succeed over the long term do so because they continuously regenerate leadership at all levels (not just because of their core competencies or use of modern management tools). Questioning leaders strengthen leaders at all levels.

Create the Motivation and Environment to Challenge the Status Quo

Successful leaders go beyond asking questions themselves; they work to create an environment in which everyone can ask and be asked questions. This means, first of all, that they focus on fostering a climate in which employees feel safe in asking questions and able to trust the system and the people involved. Without this level of safety and comfort, people are generally unwilling to be vulnerable and thus are uncomfortable with asking and answering questions that might seem threatening. And without trust and openness, people are unwilling to communicate about feelings and about problems, so they refrain from asking the leader questions that might help them.

People will not be open to questions if they feel put on the spot in being asked a question. So it is important to be careful in selecting the place and time to ask questions. The leader may need to meet individually at first, as some people may prefer not to volunteer opinions in front of a group for fear of criticism. Their questions and responses may be more candid in private. People are often more comfortable on their own turf. Questioning them in their own work setting may put them at ease and enable them to speak more freely. Later on, they may be more confident and trusting and will be more comfortable in asking and answering questions in the company of others.

People will also feel put on the spot if questions are too abrupt or accusatory—or if an immediate answer is demanded. Remember the guidelines provided in Chapter 5: ask questions out of a genuine desire to learn, in a positive manner, and give people time to respond.

If we really want to create an environment that is safe for questions, we must be committed to the growth of people. People should be seen as having an intrinsic value beyond their tangible contributions as workers. The questioning leader is deeply committed to the personal, professional, and spiritual growth of each and every individual. This includes not only promoting their learning but also taking a personal interest in their ideas and suggestions and encouraging their involvement in decision making. When leaders demonstrate this personal interest, they help create a safe environment for questions.

Leaders can demonstrate their tolerance, even encouragement, for challenging the status quo through the use of dialogue. Dialogue is a form of communication that balances advocating and inquiring. Dialogue is based on the principle that the human mind is capable of using logic and reason to understand the world, rather than having to rely on the interpretation of someone who claims authority through force, tradition, superior intellect, or divine right. Dialogue allows the group to tap the collective wisdom of its members and to see the situation as a collective whole rather than as fragmented parts. In dialogue there is an emphasis on asking questions rather than posing solutions, on gaining shared meaning rather than imposing one's own meaning. Dialogue requires trust.

Dialogue involves a relationship built on trusting, caring questions; when practiced well and often, dialogue builds trust, as people see that their questions and observations are appreciated. Central to the concept of dialogue is the idea that through the interaction, people acknowledge the wholeness of others—not just their utility. The focus is on acquiring greater understanding and attaining shared meaning. As Mark Thornhill says, questions help the employee culture move from disenfranchisement to ownership.

Isaacs notes that dialogue is more than a set of techniques for improving organizations, enhancing communications, building consensus, or solving problems. It is based on the principle that conception and implementation are intimately linked, with a core of common meaning. During the dialogue process, "people learn to think together—not just in the sense of analyzing a shared problem or creating new pieces of shared knowledge, but in the sense of occupying a collective sensibility, in which the thoughts, emotions and resulting actions belong not to one individual, but to all of them together."[6] Through dialogue people can begin to move into coordinated patterns of action and start to act in an aligned way. They can begin to see how to fit parts into a larger whole.

When you engage in dialogue, you should make sure every person's ideas are listened to and respected by other members of the group. Encourage participants to suspend criticism and analysis in the process of creatively exploring issues and problems. Respectful listening affirms people's person-to-person relationships and acknowledges the group's collective right and intellectual capacity to make sense of the world. Out of this social sharing of knowledge emerges a common pool of information and the seeds of innovation—new and imaginative insights that may lead to unexpected but valuable ideas.

When we encourage dialogue, we affirm the intellectual capability not only of the individual but also of the team and organization. We acknowledge that people are all, to some degree, blind to their own tacit assumptions and need the help of others to see them. We make it clear that each person, no matter how smart or capable—and this includes the positional leader—sees the world from a separate perspective and that other legitimate perspectives could inform that view. Wheatley points out how questions and dialogue have the potential to create "great webs" that help bring the organization together, whereas statements may create more divisiveness for the organization.[7]

Make Sure Values and Processes Do Not Conflict with Questions

Some organizational values may hinder the development of a questioning culture. Some organizations, for example, place a high value on loyalty. Many people interpret loyalty as not questioning anything said by the leader. An organization espousing loyalty as a value needs to be clear about what sort of loyalty it is promoting. Loyalty to the organization, or to the truth, may not hamper a questioning culture. When loyalty is focused on supporting the current leadership, however, a questioning culture may be impossible.

Through questions, leaders can engage their constituents in a dialogue about values. Ask them: do our values support questions? If they do, have we really been living our values? If they do not, should we reexamine them and perhaps find more appropriate values?

Kouzes and Posner note that the quest for leadership is also an inner quest to discover who you are.[8] Learning to lead is about discovering what you care about and what you value. On an organizational level, the same is true. Organizations with a questioning culture are on a quest to discover who they really are, what they are capable of, and what they can be great at.

Here are some important questions for people in organizations to wrestle with together on an ongoing basis:

- What inspires us?
- What challenges us?
- What encourages us?
- How certain are we of our conviction about the vision and the values?
- What gives us courage to continue in the face of uncertainty and adversity?
- How will we handle disappointments, mistakes, and setbacks?
- What are our strengths and weaknesses?
- What do we need to do to improve our abilities to move the organization forward?
- How solid are our relationships among ourselves?
- How can we keep ourselves motivated and encouraged?
- How prepared are we to handle the complex problems that confront our organization?
- What are our beliefs about how people ought to conduct the affairs of our organization?
- Where do we think the organization ought to be headed over the next ten years?

Asking these questions will help everyone—a team, a department, an entire organization—discover who they really are and what they really value as a group.

A common understanding of values comes about through such dialogue. Organizational values should emerge from a process, not from a pronouncement. If your organization has a formal statement of values, consider engaging people in discussing it, asking how each value affects the organization's ability to develop a questioning culture.

Standard operating procedures can also hamper the creation of a questioning culture. For example, an organization that requires layers of review and approval for even small decisions is telling employees that they are not trusted to think on their own. These employees know that their views are considered unimportant—and so their questions will be unwelcome.

Optimize the Opportunities to Ask Questions

We all have many opportunities throughout the day to ask questions. Unasked questions represent windows not opened and viewpoints and vistas not explored—unexploited opportunities to build and strengthen a questioning culture. Leaders who ask questions whenever and wherever they can have the possibility, according to James Collins, of leading companies from being good to being great.[9]

Too often, we fail to ask questions because we are in a rush. Deliberation is not rewarded in today's organizations, which prize decisiveness and action. When we rush through an agenda at a meeting, or tell people to hurry up with decisions, we are squeezing out the possibility of questions. As DuPont's Chad Holliday told me, "DuPont has over six thousand managers, each of whom must make four or five decisions each day. If we can get them to ask the right questions before they take action, DuPont will save a tremendous amount of money and time." Wheatley suggests that the most important question leaders might ask themselves concerns creating more time for questions such as these:

- How willing are people to work together to get something to work?
- What has happened to my reflection time?
- Are people willing to turn to me when confronted with conflict, grief, pain?
- Where do I see more opportunity for thought?[10]

Sometimes it is easy to find opportunities to ask questions. Says Gidget Hopf of Goodwill, "When someone comes in to see me with a problem or question, I always try to turn it around and ask them what *they* think about the problem." Most leaders certainly should be asking questions much more frequently and in more situations than they probably are doing presently. Of course, the timing of questions should be based on the context of the situation. Here are some of the occasions when questions are appropriate:

- Problem-solving sessions
- Planning meetings with employees
- Performance appraisals
- Orientations with new employees
- Staff meetings
- Discussions with customers
- Board and organization-wide meetings
- Public and community meetings

Of course, there are many more. Part Three discusses in detail how to incorporate questions into a wide variety of organizational activities.

Reward and Appreciate Questioners

Appreciation has to do with recognition, with valuing, and with gratitude. Leaders who build questioning cultures recognize the best in people and the world around them and seek to affirm past and present strengths, successes, assets, and potentials of their people. They look for opportunities to increase the value of the person and the organization. We should thus model a style of inquiry that is constructive rather than criticizing. Leaders who are fully affirmative with their people tend to be more affirmative in the questions they ask. Such questions generate more hopeful and positive responses.

While assessing what their employees have accomplished, too often leaders feel they aren't doing their jobs unless they point out the dreaded "areas for improvement." A compassionate and appreciative leadership relationship allows employees to make mistakes and learn from them. As competition increases and business environments change, organizations need employees who are willing to learn. To promote learning, employees must be allowed to make mistakes. Fear of being punished for making mistakes will cause employees to play it safe, avoid risks, and thus be unable to help the company succeed.

Empathy enables the leader to connect with those questioned. Workers need to be accepted and recognized for their special and unique personalities. A leader should assume the good intentions of coworkers and not reject them as people, even when forced to reject their behavior or performance. Those who find individuals a pain and a nuisance may be respected or feared, but they will not be willingly followed.

Questioning leaders respect each person and show concern for the well-being of all their colleagues. They want everyone to succeed and to learn from their success. This ability to empathize and be supportive is very important. Leaders should see colleagues and staff as capable of much more than they presently do—of being able to generate "beyond what anyone could imagine." These attitudes develop more trust toward the leader as well as more openness among the group of colleagues and subordinates.

Slow the Pace and the Pressure

David Rock, director of the NeuroLeadership Institute, has spent much of his life examining how the brain works and how it is affected by questions and reflection. David notes that when managers and leaders are trying to solve problems, they often throw resources at the issue, pour another cup of coffee, or—worst of all—bring a crowd of people together in an attempt to brainstorm. This is the opposite of what the brain needs. Managers have the responsibility of creating an environment in which their employees have the space to figure out the answers to questions. David says that the "better approach to thinking as a collective unit is to define a question as a group, then for individuals to take time out and do something interesting but repetitive and simple for a while, and allow your nonconscious brain to do the solving for you."

Provide Training in Questioning

Encourage fresh questions by highlighting the benefits of questions and the tragedies caused when crucial questions were not asked (such as the *Titanic*, *Challenger*, and Bay of Pigs stories in

Chapter 1). Share stories and case examples of how and when questions changed teams and organizations. Present some of the hows and whys of building a culture for questions, learning, and innovation, using this book as a resource. Resource C at the end of the book provides further ideas on training people in the art of asking questions.

HANDLING RESISTANCE TO A QUESTIONING CULTURE

Creating a culture of asking can be difficult, however, because the corporate telling culture is intangible yet pervasive. As Eric Charoux, executive director of DCDM Business School in Mauritius, told me, "Leading through asking of questions is a culture change that is not easy to bring about—we often prefer to talk with exclamation marks than with interrogation ones!"

The leader who begins to use questioning style and to encourage the organizational culture to welcome and appreciate questions is likely to meet two kinds of resistance. The first comes from people who are taken aback by a leader who starts asking questions more regularly, who are used to having the leader tell them answers instead of ask them questions. These people have *answer dependency*. The second comes from other leaders in the organization who are uncomfortable in adopting a questioning style themselves, who see their source of power as stemming from giving answers. These people have *telling dependency*.

Dealing with Answer Dependency

A leader who begins to ask questions on a regular basis should be aware that people may not understand or trust this new way of operating. If the leader's role has been to solve problems, provide information, and have all the answers, a change to a questioning style will usually cause those who have become dependent on the leader to feel abandoned. They may feel that the leader has some sort of secret agenda, or that the leader is only asking questions to catch them on something. How should the leader handle these concerns and perhaps skepticism? Clarke-Epstein recommends that leaders new to using questioning be honest and up-front.[11] Tell those you lead that you have been rethinking your leadership style and that one of the things you are exploring is the value of being a leader who asks questions. This way, listeners are prepared when you ask questions, and you reassure them that you have no ulterior motive. You can also go a long way toward lessening resistance among those with answer dependency by following the guidelines set out here and in Chapter 5.

If you ask empowering questions from a sincere desire to learn rather than blame, give people the time to respond at their own pace, listen to responses openly and nonjudgmentally, and follow up on the conversation with action; then people will gradually learn that they have not been abandoned and that no hidden agenda is in the works. Moreover, if you set the example, provide a safe environment for questioning and challenging the status quo, and appreciate and reward questioners, you will gradually wean people from their answer dependency.

In addition, it is probably wise to move ahead slowly, according to Mark Harper of ConocoPhillips:

> If I were going through this change in leadership style again, there are a few things I would do differently. I made a rather

abrupt change in style at the start and went from one extreme of making decisions to the other of asking a lot of questions and making few decisions. The lesson I learned is that a slower change and a better balance might have been more effective.

Dealing with Telling Dependency

For all the reasons discussed in Chapter 3, other managers in your department or organization may see the move to a questioning culture as undercutting their authority. They may have built their careers on technical competence, on being right, and thus see moving to questions as a direct attack on what has made them successful. Saying "*I don't know,*" as Alan Wurtzel did, may just be too threatening. Others may resist the whole idea of using questions because they see it as giving up control. Sometimes they fear that asking questions may bring them unwelcome information.

People don't resist change so much as they resist *being changed*. In other words, the way to get others to adopt a questioning leadership style is to ask them to do so rather than tell them to do so. Telling people rather than asking lays the foundation for defensiveness and resistance because it does thrust change upon them, and this is especially true when the telling involves informing people how they personally need to change. Why? When we tell someone what to do differently and why it is important to do it, we convey subtle—even if unintended—messages along with the information; messages like "My way is better" and "You are weak; your way is wrong."

So the inquiring leader will try to get other leaders in the organization to also lead with questions by asking questions.

Consider, too, steering the managers on your team away from the all-too-common idea that if you don't assert yourself with strong statements, you will not be respected. In *Just Ask Leadership*, Gary Cohen cites research showing that 95 percent of employees prefer to be asked questions rather than be told what to do.[12] Involving employees and colleagues in decision-making processes builds an environment rich with energy, excitement, and innovative problem solving. When you ask questions, you show respect—and in turn you are respected. It is that simple, says Cohen.

Here are some questions to ask to help others see the value of leading with questions and embracing a questioning culture:

- Would you like people to solve their own problems rather than come to you?
- How do you feel when I ask you questions?
- Why do you think the idea of leading with questions makes you uncomfortable?

Use these and similar questions as a way to engage in dialogue, not to score points or engage in a debate. If you actually meet resistance to these questions, the best response is to stay quiet. You have to give people time to think. The listener has to process everything about why you are now asking questions and then go through the process of formulating the answer. We sometimes forget or find it difficult to look at the world from a perspective other than our own. We see only what is important from our own perspective, which may not be what is important to someone else. People tend to resist changes that are thrust upon them; they naturally support ideas and changes that they help to create. Questions, as I have noted, pull people to a possible future. As leaders, our questions have the power to provide support rather than increase pressure on the individuals around us.

START THE JOURNEY

Perhaps one of the most important roles of a leader, according to Edgar Schein, is to create and build the culture of the organization and the groups within that organization—a corporate culture with values and behaviors, with visions and basic assumptions, one that appreciates quality, risk taking, teamwork, ethical behavior, success, and results.[13] The most effective way to build this culture is derived from the questions asked by leaders—questions that inspire, clarify, energize, and both produce and resolve productive conflict.

All companies can strengthen their cultures by making them question-friendly. Leaders must model the way, promote values that support inquiry, ensure a safe environment that permits challenging the status quo, find opportunities to ask questions, reward questioners, and make training available when needed.

What else should you do to create a questioning culture? Mark Harper of ConocoPhillips says you just take the first step. "My advice to others considering using questions to lead is to start the journey. I have seen significant positive results and would recommend this methodology to anyone."

QUESTIONS FOR REFLECTION

1. What can I do to make my organization a questioning and learning organization?
2. How can I model a questioning culture with questions?
3. What values and processes in my organization conflict with a questioning culture?
4. How can I create more opportunities for others to ask questions?
5. How do I encourage and reward questioners?
6. What strategies can I use to encourage dialogue in our conversations?
7. How can we slow the pace so we can reflect and ask better questions?
8. What training in questioning skills can we offer in our organization?
9. How can I handle resistance to the use of questions?
10. How can I change the culture from dependency on "telling" to a culture that allows freedom for questions?

PART III

A Guide for Leaders on When and How to Ask Powerful Questions

Using Questions in Managing People

Each question a leader asks can provide a wonderful opportunity for the recipients to become empowered, to do something that they could not do before. Questions have the potential to create confidence, to enhance learning, to develop competence, to engender insights. Questions can move each person in the organization to become a better human being as well as a better contributor to the organization and to the community.

Ron Edmondson, pastor of Immanuel Baptist Church in Lexington, Kentucky, with over thirty years of leadership experience as a business owner and as a spiritual leader, shared with me the twelve leadership questions that he has found most useful for empowering people around him:

- What can we learn from this?
- Do you understand what I'm asking you to do?

- How can I help you?
- What's next?
- Where should we be placing our best energy?
- What are we missing or forgetting?
- How can we do it better next time?
- What do you think?
- What changes could we implement to make your work life better?
- What would you do differently if you had my position?
- Are you enjoying your work?
- How can I improve my communication with you?

In this chapter, I discuss how leaders can use questions in managing their staff—how they can use questions to strengthen their relationships with their direct reports, help them grow, and encourage action and innovative thinking. I also review the use of questions in orienting new staff members, setting goals and objectives, conducting performance appraisals, and leading staff meetings, among other topics.

BUILDING RELATIONSHIPS THAT EMPOWER

Andrew Sobel and Jerold Panas, coauthors of *Power Questions*, note that "telling creates resistance, whereas asking creates relationships."[1] Block points out that we, as leaders, can open magnificent possibilities with others when we recognize that our questioning, reflection, and conversation with others are, in themselves, important action steps.[2] Thus, even before a response from the person questioned, and even if the person does not respond, we have established a significant relationship. Through questions, leaders create a social space where authentic accountability, commitment, and community become a possibility.

As noted in Chapter 4, many leaders unfortunately ask questions that disempower rather than empower their subordinates—questions that cause reaction rather than creation. By asking disempowering questions, leaders close the gateway to identifying paths to success. *Empowering questions*, on the other hand, get people to think and allow them to discover their own answers, thus developing self-responsibility and transference of ownership for the results.

But even empowering questions don't exist in a vacuum; they need to be tailored to the individual who will answer them. Different people need different sorts of questions, depending on their personality, style of thinking, skill set, and other factors. Suzanne Milchling, head of the Department of Defense's Homeland Defense Business Unit, says it takes some experimentation to find the right questioning style with people.

> The most valuable questions for me are the ones that get the result I want. It is a trial-and-error event with everyone until I get to understand them and how they think. I use questions to match our thinking styles or strategies. For example, one scientist insists on briefing the general first because he is convinced his work has high-level merit. I agree but ask, "Have you considered briefing the chief first? With his buy-in it will be easier for the general to fund your project."

I ask probing questions because my people want to look good and I want them to look good. The goal is to get them to learn on their own. Whatever they want to accomplish is what I help them do. The questions are the catalysts for learning what's already in their minds. The abstract thinkers, like my son Robert, need to be made aware of the details. Their thinking is in patterns, and I want them to understand the "detail" thinkers—the people they may have to convince—the people who think in details and linearly.

The most valuable questions for me are those that turn people to look inward at how they are perceived by others. When I ask some of the employees, "How are you going to do the project?" I get a straight answer. Those [employees] I call *direct*; I can direct them to do something and they answer my questions in a direct and linear manner.

For other, more abstract thinkers, I need them to cycle within. Asking questions like "Would it be useful to get Jim's ideas first? Would he be able to grease the skids for you?" Getting abstract thinkers to recycle their thought patterns in slow motion and out loud to me and others raises questions within them that they may not have thought of before.

It is the question that was unanticipated and not asked that gets our people in trouble. Thus another valuable question is "What question didn't I ask myself or my employee?"

Peter Cheng, director of PACE OD in Singapore, told me about the importance of creating a sense of urgency in questions, so one can ask the types of questions that "prompt others to take ownership for getting things done for themselves and for their organizations":

During my days as marketing manager for a healthcare company, my boss asked me a question that sent shocks down my spine and increased my sense of urgency to act. It all happened when she brought me to the warehouse and made me stand right in the middle of a high pile of expiring vitamins (less than twelve months shelf-life). Any product that has less than eighteen months of shelf-life is considered "poor" quality. So when my GM asked "What are you going to do about it?" right in front of the pile of stocks, I was visibly at a loss for words. I was stirred up to act more promptly and managed to clear a fair bit of the expiring stocks and minimize expenses due to stock write-off. The lesson I learned here is that when a "disturbing" question is asked, it creates a paradigm shift and urgency to act. When combined with the visible presence of the problem at hand, asking "disturbing questions" is a powerful way to get people to act with a heightened sense of urgency.

Two questions that I now frequently use are:

1. If you do nothing about this situation, what might be some consequences/outcomes that will unfold? (This is asked of someone after helping that person think of an ideal state of affairs versus the current state of affairs.)
2. What if you are wrong? How would it affect your position? Asking what if . . . allows the person to think of the other perspective that might be possible, so that he or she is prepared to cover all grounds and have contingency plans to act, just in case.

Questions that stress values can build relationships. Whitney, Cooperrider, Trosten-Bloom, and Kaplin suggest asking value-related questions, such as, "What most attracted you to this company? What has it contributed to you and your life? How can we create more of that quality within this organization?" They also suggest questions they refer to as "best-in-class questions"—that is, questions that demonstrate levels of organizational excellence beyond the reach of other "good" organizations as well as geared to meet high levels of employee satisfaction. For example, "What is it about you and the way you do your job that's best-in-class? What effect do these skills or behavior have on your department? On the organization as a whole?"[3]

ESTABLISHING A COACHING RELATIONSHIP WITH DIRECT REPORTS

Carl Rogers, one of the most influential leaders in humanist psychology, notes that three conditions are necessary if we are to help change the person we are with: genuineness, empathetic understanding, and positive regard.[4] Roger Carkhuff suggests that three additional conditions—respect, concreteness, and self-disclosure—can further strengthen these interpersonal relationships as well as results.[5] Rogers's observations suggest that in building relationships with subordinates, our questions need to be genuine and demonstrate a learner mindset, as described in Chapter 5; our listening needs to be active and empathetic, and we should show appreciation for the responses we receive. Carkhuff's additional conditions indicate that our questions should be empowering and specific and that we should be expansive and open in responding to questions our staff members pose to us.

As noted earlier, one of the most important roles for today's leaders is to serve as coach as well as mentor to their subordinates. Mark Harper of ConocoPhillips says, "I lead with questions in my personal coaching sessions with direct reports." When we ask questions of others in a way that signals that we are partners in a discovery process intended to enrich the whole group, we build strong relationships.

Bianco-Mathis, Nabors, and Roman have developed a powerful model with the following steps for developing and carrying out this supportive coaching role with individuals we are leading.

1. Establish the relationship through reflection, learning, honesty, and determination.
2. Analyze the experience via inquiry, advocacy, resiliency, and self-management.
3. Process and seek to understand the feedback.
4. Plan actions via dialogue, reflection, problem solving, decision making, and risk taking.
5. Take action with openness, courage, and commitment to learning.
6. Continuously evaluate progress.[6]

Gidget Hopf of Goodwill explained to me how she made the transition to becoming a coach to her staff rather than just a boss:

> About four years ago I began working with an executive coach who had been very helpful in assisting me to gain increasing self-awareness about how I interact with my

leadership team. At that time, my coach and I began to discuss new ways of interacting, including asking questions rather than telling. I had always been inclined to offer solutions rather than empower people to solve their own problems. I just automatically assumed that if someone was at my door with a problem, they expected me to solve it. Through the coaching I realized how disempowering this is, and how much more effective I could be by posing the question back to the individual with the problem. This took active concentration on my part to practice this new behavior, and a lot of reinforcing by the coach.

What I came to realize is that solving others' problems is exhausting. It is much more effective to provide the opportunity for them to solve their own problems. So instead of jumping in with a quick response when someone would come to me, I began responding this way: "Well, I am sure you have had time to think about this and have your own ideas; what have you come up with?" This type of question is very validating, and lets the person know that I respect their knowledge and experience. I have come to believe that solving people's problems sends a message that you don't think they can do it themselves. Very often people have thought out their answers and just want to test them with someone else. I now give them a chance to do that.

Tom Laughlin, of the consulting firm Caravela, described three questions that he has found to be especially helpful in building relationships with his staff:

- *How can I help you?* This question has generated some phenomenal responses. It clarifies immediately what the person wants. Oftentimes, the only thing that people want is permission to execute their own strategy. Other times, they may be seeking advice or wishing to inform me.

- *What would you do?* I have found it very valuable to find out how people would respond to their own problem or to their own question.
- *What would someone else (say, a competitor) do?*

Good leaders regard every encounter as an opportunity to coach. A key skill of coaching is the art of questioning. Asking incisive questions inspires people to think, to discover, to search.

FOSTERING REFLECTION AND LEARNING

Reflection involves recalling, thinking about, pulling apart, making sense, and trying to understand. Cultivating the ability to reflect can help generate tremendous personal, intellectual, psychological, and social growth. Reflection helps people experience "breakthrough learning" when they become aware of the need to reach beyond their conscious beliefs and challenge their assumptions about their present worldview. Questions that encourage reflection are the key to significant learning—or what Mezirow calls *transformative* learning.[7] Questions enable individuals to gain both double-loop learning (why something occurs) and triple-loop learning (what in the system causes the something to occur).

Reflection increases self-awareness, which helps people relate to others more genuinely. When we ask others to reflect, to look within, it can help us understand them on a deeper level. In other words, when others understand themselves more fully, they can reveal themselves to us in a more robust way. Robert Hoffman of Novartis provides a telling example:

> I remember working with one outstanding person with whom I would struggle over issues and strategies. He had assumptions that were very different from mine. I soon realized how useful it was to ask him questions and to find out about his underlying thinking. I asked questions such as, "*What was going on in your head when you did this? What values caused these actions?*" These questions led to trust and the development of a good working relationship.

Hoffman was having trouble understanding his colleague. He used questions to encourage the colleague to reflect, which led to Hoffman's having a better understanding of the other person. Of course, a trusting relationship is important when we ask people to reflect and reveal to us the insights they discover.

Mike Stice, who has had nearly thirty years in the gas and oil business, told me that the questions he found to be most useful are open-ended questions such as "How did you arrive at that conclusion?" Or "When did you first realize that your action was required?" "These types of questions," he notes, "allow me to observe the respondent's thought process and uncover the sequence of events that led to a particular decision or action."

Whitney and colleagues suggest the following questions as very valuable in generating reflection, learning, and career development:

- How do you learn best?
- How did you foster your own development?

- What made this a high-point learning experience?
- What were the most challenging and exciting career development opportunities that you have experienced?
- What made it challenging and exciting?
- How did you benefit?
- How did the organization benefit?[8]

Of course, we need to help ourselves reflect as well. According to James Champy, "Great achievers learn to temper their ambition with self-reflection. They remain true to their values, see the world (and themselves) clearly, and effectively manage the resources that can limit the pursuit of a dream—time, talent, and momentum."[9]

Questions challenge one's programmed knowledge, or what Schein refers to as "theories in use."[10] Reflective inquiry generates dialogue and mutual support for each other, as questions require us to listen. Bass points out that changes in attitudes, assumptions, and values require reflection on the individual's own mental models.[11] Without self-awareness of mental models, it is impossible for a person to change.

Peter and Lily Cheng, whose Singapore-based company trains leaders on how to ask better questions, have developed a list of questions that can be effective in various scenarios:

1. Can-do questions, to use when subordinates lack confidence, run out of ideas in doing a task, or are showing poor work performance
2. Gap-analysis questions, to employ when there is a need to determine what is required of employees to achieve desired performance goals

161

3. Engaging questions, to use when people do not "buy" your idea

4. Reframing questions, which enable leaders to help people to move from complaining about something to seeing new possibilities

5. Advising questions, which can be used when people ask for advice or when the leader detects competency or knowledge gaps

6. Action questions, which are powerful and encourage action and commitment

ENCOURAGING ACTION AND INNOVATION

Questions transform problem- and possibility-talk into action as they move people from the present to the future. Marilee Goldberg remarks that questions are the primary means by which doing, having, accomplishing, and growing are catalyzed—and often even made manifest—in our lives.[12] Because questions are intrinsically related to action, they spark and direct attention, perception, energy, and effort, and so are at the heart of the evolving forms that our lives assume. Mark Harper of ConocoPhillips uses a variety of questions to spur innovation and activity:

- What is a viable alternative?
- What are the advantages and disadvantages you see in this suggestion?
- Can you more fully describe your concerns?
- What are your goals?
- What is the current reality?

- What are a few options for improvement?
- What will you commit to do, by when?

To encourage innovation and action, leaders should encourage people to think about their own solutions, instead of giving them solutions to problems. Ask questions such as "What do you think is the real problem?" or "If you proceed in that direction, what are the possible consequences?"

Questions can, as Peter Vaill observes, open people to the possibility that they are capable of spontaneously generating astonishing new material, material that goes far beyond what anyone imagined was possible.[13] Gary Hamel, chairman of the innovation consulting firm Strategos, says that innovators typically view the world through four lenses: they look for deeply held conventions and challenge them; they look for change in the world and understand the revolutionary potential of the change; they empathize with customers and anticipate their needs; and they view their organizations less like businesses and more like skill sets, constantly asking, "How do I creatively recombine what I know to make new things?"[14]

Jean-Paul Gaillard is president of the Ethical Coffee Company. He previously served as CEO of Movenpick Foods and Nestlé USA as well as marketing manager of Philip Morris Europe and Warner Electric. Based on his many years as a senior manager, Jean-Paul has developed a number of insights and strategies on how he would ask questions that boost productivity, and thereby encourage action: "Questions should be tough on oneself as well as others. When people are challenged, they give more than less. Questions can get people's emotions going. With my questions, I like to get people to aim high."

Jean-Paul emphasized to me that it is "important to stretch people, but not too far. Questions should create challenging opportunities. They should be open-ended but focused so as not to dilute their impact and benefit. Great questions that are targeted can enable people to surpass their current levels of productivity and even their expectations."

Bossidy and Charan note that one of the most important roles of the leader is to create the next generation of leaders.[15] As Pentti Sydänmaanlakka, a former HR director at Nokia, said to me, "Leadership is . . . inspiring and showing others new places where they haven't been earlier. Good leadership is showing the way to self-leadership." Frances Hesselbein, chairman of the Board of Governors of the Leader to Leader Institute, agrees: "Building a sustainable organization is one of a leader's primary responsibilities. When the challenges of today have been met, will your organization have the vigor to grow tomorrow?" Two keys to building sustainable organizations, she says, are grooming successors, "not a chosen one but a pool of gifted potential leaders," and "dispersing the tasks of leadership across the organization until there are leaders at every level."[16]

Asking questions and helping people feel in control of their own lives is a key factor in creating leadership capabilities within each person. Asking people what they think encourages them to expand their opportunities to develop ideas, to be listened to, to test out actions.

Jeff Carew of Collectcorp told me, "Employees, specifically your direct reports, need to have an opportunity to learn from you—learn everything about your job—if they are one day going to take on more responsibility—preferably some of your current responsibilities—to allow them and yourself to grow."

"What have you done today to develop your leadership skills?" is a question frequently asked by Neal Anderson of TESOL.[17] Executive coach Isabel Rimanoczy says that she helps people grow and become leaders "by focusing on questions rather than on answers." Too often employees focus on leaders, looking to them for answers, as if leaders were the source of all knowledge. "We put the focus on them, trusting their knowledge and wisdom. And, even when they did not think they had answers, they dived into themselves for the answers, and—not surprisingly—they always found the answers." She adds, "A deep transformation . . . had taken place in those individuals because they had increased their self-awareness and realized that there was wisdom inside them that could be unearthed with questions."

MANAGING KEY EMPLOYEE INTERACTIONS

As leaders, we meet with our staff informally quite often. But in addition to these daily interactions in the course of work, we also have more structured and formal interactions, involving new hires, performance reviews, and the like. Questions can make these sometimes bureaucratic sessions more powerful than fill-in-the-blanks routines.

Questions for Planning and Setting Objectives

Leaders should meet regularly with staff to discuss projects, activities, concerns, and issues. Too often these meetings are set up with statements such as "report to me by three o'clock on Friday." In planning and setting objectives, the leader could ask some of the following types of questions, which can all act as springboards to better, more effective action:

- What do we need to accomplish?
- What do you think is realistic?
- How are you planning to accomplish this objective?
- What resources are you looking for?
- What kind of help do you need?

In checking progress toward goals, you can inspire better work by asking your colleague a series of nonthreatening questions, such as these:

- Are you still on track to have that report finished by Friday afternoon?
- Do you have all the information that you need?
- Would it be useful for us to go through some aspects of the report?

Such questions cause people to reflect on the goal you are after and also to anticipate what needs to be done. If there are problems or potential misunderstandings, asking nonthreatening questions provides an opportunity to uncover and address potential pitfalls before the action is completed.[18]

Cargill's Douglas Eden says, "Effective questions for me relate to goals. I often ask questions such as 'What are your goals for this year? What is really driving you this year? What would it look like if you achieved that goal?' Discovering one's goals can help one to prioritize, to become aware of inconsistencies among goals, to help develop great relationships."

166

Leeds identifies a number of other types of questions that can be introduced during sessions to set plans and determine strategies:

- *To call attention to a point*: Why do you think John found it difficult to accept this challenge?
- *To get information*: What is the best way to get there from here?
- *To uncover causes or relationships*: How has the conflict with Bob affected progress on this project?
- *To test ideas*: Suppose we did it this way? What would happen?
- *To keep the discussion to the point*: Can we go back to [whatever the original focus was]?
- *To bring out opinions and attitudes*: How do we feel about this?
- *To bring out reactions to a point made*: How do you feel about this?
- *To suggest an action, idea, or decision*: What do you think the results would be if you did [something]?[19]

Determining the place and time of asking questions of those who are reluctant to respond to inquiry is important. As noted in Chapter 6, you may need to ask questions in private at first to make things easier for people who prefer not to volunteer opinions in front of a group. After a while, they may become more confident and trusting, more comfortable in asking and answering questions regardless of the setting.

Questions During Performance Appraisals

Performance appraisals have become such a horrible experience for both the supervisor and the employee that they are dreaded by both parties. Most of us would rather skip these appraisals than conduct them. The appropriate questions, however, can make these events more productive—even actually enjoyable. Sue Whitt of Abbott Laboratories, who served as senior vice president of Worldwide Development Operations for Pfizer's global R&D business as well as vice president of Worldwide Technical Operations for Parke-Davis, encourages the use of questions in performance appraisals: "With my staff, I found that questions are equally applicable and essential for improving performance. Questions during performance appraisal sessions can be very powerful as they can be individualized. Through my questions, they could see how their behaviors were counter-productive to what they wanted to achieve."

Clarke-Epstein, in her research on great questions for leaders, received suggestions such as the following, which would be very effective to ask employees during performance appraisal sessions:

- How does your work contribute to our success?
- How could you make your job more effective?
- Who do you see as our competitors, and how do you see them?
- What gets in the way of doing your job?
- What does our leadership team do that gets in the way of your job?
- How could we communicate management decisions more effectively?
- If you could change one thing about the organization, what would it be?
- What's a potential benefit that we could offer that would be helpful to you?

- What is it like to work on a team in our organization?
- What makes you proud to work for this organization?
- What's something you've learned in the past week?
- What brings you joy in your work?
- What gives your life meaning?[20]

Questions such as these might even be given to the employee beforehand so that the performance appraisal becomes a dialogue that results in actions and learning that benefit all parties—the employee, the supervisor, and the organization as a whole.

David Smyk, who has more than twenty years' experience in major firms, says that there is always one more question to ask. "One of the most powerful questions is one that I ask at the end: *'Are there any questions that I have not asked you that I should have asked you and, if so, can we discuss them now?'* You wouldn't believe the additional information I am able to obtain in most cases."

Jeanette Partlow, president of the Maryland Chemical Company, says she uses questions like these extensively in performance reviews:

- What is your goal?
- What was your performance?
- Is there a gap?
- What caused the gap (either positive or negative)?
- Based on this information: For next month, to close a negative gap or preserve a positive difference, what will you keep doing, start doing, and stop doing?

Giving Feedback

By the nature of the performance appraisal process, many leaders may feel compelled to give what they fondly think of as "constructive" feedback rather than ask positive questions. If constructive feedback is needed, the best approach is to ask people what *they* think should be worked on. In most situations, employees are very aware of their shortcomings. When those areas are enumerated by the employee, you can suggest working on the one or two you think would be most beneficial to improve on. This keeps you in the realm of coaching, not judging. According to Pentti Sydänmaanlakka, using questions is especially powerful when giving feedback:

> When giving feedback there are some basic rules, and the first one is that people should first give their own corrective feedback. Usually they are then quite open and critical. Then when you are giving your corrective feedback, you should do it using questions like: "Do you think your performance was optimal in this case? Do you see any ways to improve your performance? What things would you do differently if you could start the project once again?"
>
> People themselves should seek to gain insights relative to their strengths and weaknesses. It is better that they understand them first; they should tell them to you—not vice versa, as is usually the case. Depending on the situation, I have found the following questions to be most effective:
>
> - *Inquiring*: Why did you do it in this way? What should we actually do?
> - *Concretizing*: Can you give some examples?

170

- *Exploring*: Can you say some more about why you have come to this conclusion?
- *Challenging*: Don't you see any other way to do this?
- *Coaching*: What did you learn in that process?
- *Reorienting*: What is actually our problem? Can you find a totally different approach to it?
- *Summarizing*: Can we agree about this? How would you summarize your solution?

Encouraging People to Ask and Respond to Questions

Because of the high-stakes and stressful nature of typical performance reviews, we should not be overly surprised when employees are reluctant to ask questions or uncomfortable in answering questions addressed to them. Your staff also may doubt whether you are truly interested in what they think, and they may fear that their answers may be wrong, dumb, or unacceptable.

Marshall Goldsmith has found the following advice valuable in getting employees to open up and to ask or answer questions. Goldsmith suggests that the leader have a conversation built around six discussion points, starting each conversation by describing them so that the other person doesn't feel set up or trapped in a game of "guess what the leader wants." Each of these questions can help people understand what you are trying to teach and achieve. Leaders should carefully consider the impact of each question.

1. *Where are we going?* I will tell you where I think we're going; you tell me where you think we're going.

171

2. *Where are you going?* I'll tell you where I see you going; you tell me where you see yourself going.

3. *What are you doing well?* I'll give you my sense of what you're doing well; you give me your sense of what you're doing well.

4. *What suggestions for improvement do you have for yourself?* I'll tell you what suggestions I have; you tell me what suggestions you have.

5. *How can I help you?* I'll add anything else I think I can do; you tell me what I can do to help and support you.

6. *What suggestions do you have for me?* I'll tell you what I think I need to do; you tell me what you think I need to do.[21]

When done well, performance appraisals do not have to be exercises in accusation and denial. Questions are the key to making appraisals learning opportunities for both the supervisor and the employee.

Questions for New Employees

Early days on the job are excellent opportunities for the leader to help a new employee feel comfortable in the new environment and have confidence in the organization's leadership, to show interest and commitment to their ideas, and to inspire and encourage the individual to take actions. Some of the following questions would be valuable during these first days:

- Why did you decide to work for us?
- How would you describe our organization?
- What's one great question I could ask someone new (or an old hand, a customer, and so on)?

- What questions can I answer for you?
- What do you need to learn—both in terms of skills and people to know?
- What would you like to be doing in five years?

Clarke-Epstein suggests that those who bring in new leaders ask them some of the following questions:

- Why do you think we made you a new leader?
- What did the greatest leader you ever had do?
- What do you need to learn to be a great leader?
- How can we support you to grow as a leader?[22]

And when you become a new leader, it represents the perfect opportunity to use your naive understandings to your advantage. At that stage, colleagues are more tolerant of your dumb questions (or what Revans would call *fresh* questions). It is easier to ask why the organization does this or that, or to ask employees what really bugs them about the organization. Here's one great question for the new leader to ask subordinates: What gets in the way of doing the best job possible?

A FINAL WORD

Using questions can help you to become a better leader and generate stronger results from your staff. But it has another benefit. Questioning your colleagues can help them become questioners as well, individuals who generate a questioning insight as a way of life. Jayan Warrier, director of Latitude Leadership and codirector of the World Institute for Action

Learning–Singapore, told me how one powerful question began a personal transformation:

> Several years ago, I was working as an engineer in a large corporation and was asked to join a three-month leadership program. I seemed to not be making much progress in life beyond the tasks assignments given to me. I was like a smart student who comes up first in my class, but unhappy and who has lost touch with the self. My group leader, who was becoming impatient with me, looked into my eyes and asked: "Do you consider yourself successful in life so far?" I did not know how to respond to that question and did not have an immediate response. That question, however, triggered many more questions within me about what life and the definition of success should mean for me. It was the beginning of many changes I made in my life, which were sometimes painful but rewarding. I would consider this question priceless to me.

Vaill points out that self-awareness and astute understanding of personal motives are the most critical of all leadership skills.[23] Enabling and equipping people to become reflective practitioners will help them become better leaders. This readiness to change and grow via questions is a prerequisite for development.

QUESTIONS FOR REFLECTION

1. How can I empower people with questions?
2. How can I use questions to foster reflection and learning among my colleagues and subordinates?

3. What questions can I ask to help others to better solve their own problems?

4. How can I get more action and energy with my questions?

5. What questions will build leadership skills in me and others?

6. What are the best questions for planning and setting objectives?

7. What questions should I ask during performance appraisals?

8. What would be the best questions to help new employees?

9. How can I give feedback with questions?

10. What questions would generate more creativity?

Using Questions to Build Teams

Teams now dominate organizational life, from senior executive teams and cross-functional teams to project teams, virtual teams, and more. Peter Senge remarks that teams have become a critical component of every enterprise and are now the predominant unit for decision making and getting things done.[1] Tom Peters points out how the critical work of organizations will need to be done in groups—due to the demands of customers, speed, learning, and efficiency.[2] Long ago, Margaret Mead, the world-famous anthropologist, noted that we should "never underestimate the power of a small group with dedication to change the world; it is, in fact, the only thing that does."

But teams are not without their problems. Margaret Wheatley observes that in too many organizations *team* is a four-letter word.[3] Unfortunately, most groups are ineffective when first formed, and many never improve thereafter.

Members of many teams and groups are frustrated by the ineffective productivity of their group and the painful social interactions and storming that occur within it.

For many of us, team meetings are emblematic of the problems with teams. Too often, meetings are held with fixed agendas and little time for questions or open-ended discussions. Not much gets accomplished, and agreed-to tasks are frequently not implemented. Communications are strained, one-way, and often overtly or covertly hostile. Even when meetings have a clear agenda, the overall purpose of the meeting can be obscure. All too often team meetings sap energy and enthusiasm when they should leave people feeling energized, with a clear direction and eagerness to move ahead.

In this chapter, I discuss how leaders can use questions to improve team functioning, solve problems, and resolve conflict.

LEADING TEAMS AS A COACH-QUESTIONER

Bianco-Mathis, Nabors, and Roman distinguish between how a traditional leader leads a team and how a coaching leader behaves; that is, between a leader who tells and a leader who questions.[4] The traditional leader focuses on control, seeks to minimize risk, and pushes to be the initiator of action. Such a leader tends to give commands via statements, control change, hoard information, and foreclose debate. From the traditional perspective, the team exists for the convenience of the leader. The result is a group that achieves limited development, remains dependent on the leader, asks few questions, and accomplishes relatively little.

In contrast, the leader who coaches with questions sees the team as having an independent existence in its own right, serving a larger organizational purpose. Such a team has the potential to grow continuously. A coaching, questioning leader develops a group that possesses and demonstrates a culture of trust, support, and open discussion. In this type of leadership, the leader reminds people of their capabilities and strengths and that they are more likely to continue to build their power as a group. Exhibit 8.1 illustrates the differences between these two types of group leaders.

Exhibit 8.1. Traditional and Coaching Leaders' Behavior and Legacies

Traditional Leader Behaviors with Team	Legacy	Coaching Leader Behaviors with Team	Legacy
Focus on containing and controlling.	Limited development.	Focus on expanding and facilitating.	Team continues to redefine itself and grow.
Initiates action.	Team follows directions and waits until told.	Holds self and team accountable for initiating actions.	Team values keeping promises and performing as promised.

(continued)

Exhibit 8.1 (*continued*)

Traditional Leader Behaviors with Team	Legacy	Coaching Leader Behaviors with Team	Legacy
Minimizes risk at expense of timely action.	Bias toward inaction and using only tried-and-true methods.	Facilitates acting with speed and flexibility; pushes for creative solutions.	Bias toward action—team routinely takes calculated risks.
Gives commands.	Team doesn't participate, raise questions, or suggest alternatives.	Consults with team regarding problems and solutions.	Team uses a helping stance—recognizes handoff and opportunities for support—learns how to work toward solutions independently.
Establishes boss-subordinate relationship with team.	People are defined and limited by their positions.	Establishes partnership with team.	Team members are engaged and accountable.

Hoards information and knowledge.	Discourages responsibility and trust.	Shares knowledge and information.	Encourages responsibility and builds trust.
Tries to dictate or control change.	Team members display resistance, fear, and poor performance.	Tries to lead and plan for change collaboratively.	Team accepts change as way of life— displays resilience and adaptability.

Mark Harper of ConocoPhillips went through two mergers in quick succession. His story of how he put together a team in a difficult postmerger environment illustrates how a coaching and questioning approach can build teams:

Two years ago, following a second merger in less than a year, I was struggling to get my management team aligned and fully engaged. Following the first of those two mergers, only about half of this team seemed to be truly committed to the new organization, and I was looking for a new way to lead my group out of this second merger. At about the same time, I participated in a 360-degree feedback process and received some personal coaching from some consultants who were

181

helping me to initiate a Balanced Scorecard management process.

The coaches introduced me to a method of leadership coaching called the GROW model, based on the work of John Whitmore.[5] The GROW model suggests that coaching is best accomplished through the use of effective questions. Those questions help to focus people on their *Goals*, current *Reality*, *Options* for improvement, and finally on *What* they will commit to do to improve.

The impact of using questions like these has been to get people to open up and put more of their concerns on the table. This has had many positive results. There have been so many positive changes that I am amazed that only eight months after merger closure, it is hard to imagine that we could have accomplished as much in any other way. A few of those changes include the following:

- A more aligned management team
- A clearly defined vision and strategy
- A culture that no longer talks about the "old way"
- An energized organization
- A new business model
- New brand and imaging positioning

The bottom-line impact on the organization includes targeted merger synergies that have been achieved and exceeded, employee morale improvement, reduction in operating expenses, and solid sales volumes during a difficult economy.

Similarly, Sue Whitt talked to me about putting together a new team after a merger between Pfizer and Warner-Lambert:

182

I asked people to move their personal agendas. Different people were needed to design and develop different parts of our merger with Warner-Lambert. We had to learn how to interact. I remember how we were all looking around at each other at the table. No one knew what roles each would have. I quickly recognized that people were more receptive to using questions. Everyone needed to learn in order to do the task. Being able to ask good questions was essential. As a result of our questioning and collaboration, our bosses were very impressed, noting that the team was so effective, laughing and working—and not fighting like the other teams.

Mark Harper says that he uses questions in four ways in leading his team:

One use involves encouraging people to see things from a different perspective. Surfacing and changing unconscious biases is very important in a postmerger environment. A second use involves getting all the issues on the table. Many times I have sensed that I wasn't hearing all of the concerns that existed, and the careful use of questioning helped me to surface those concerns. A third way that I use questions is to get everyone engaged in important issues, either in meetings or in one-on-one situations. And finally, I lead with questions in my personal coaching sessions with direct reports.

As Harper's and Whitt's experiences demonstrate, a leader can strengthen a team in a multitude of ways by asking questions of the group and encouraging others to ask questions as well. Skillfully using and encouraging questions can help you achieve a number of specific goals:

- *A shared commitment to solving problems*. To help the members realize that they are accountable and that they must work together if they are going to be successful, ask, "*How has this problem affected us? What help do we need? How can we improve our communication and collaboration? Who else has something to contribute on this topic?*"

- *Alignment around clear values and goals*. To help people jointly clarify the goal and achieve agreement on what the group should do, ask, "*What are we trying to achieve? Who has a different view? What's the ultimate purpose behind this goal?*" Use questions to remind members not to assume that everyone automatically agrees on the goal of the group, and that consensus on a goal is possible only if they ask questions of each other.

- *Willingness to work with others to develop strategies*. In many groups, the members have been thrust into problems and situations entirely new to them (especially if the team has sought members who may have fresh questions as well as individuals who have experience with the issue). To remind people that no one in the group will have all the answers, ask, "*What is marketing's perspective on this? What is manufacturing's perspective? Who else has something to add? How can we bring these different views together? Have we thought of all possible options?*"

- *Improved morale*. David Smyk told me, "Don't underestimate how one can also use questions to increase morale. For example, '*What can the rest of the team do to help you on this project?*' When people know you want them to succeed and you are willing to put your work aside to help them, they tend to perform better and do so with less stress."

• *Clear and accepted norms.* To help establish unique and strong group norms, norms that are powerfully ingrained and provide strong cohesion for the group, ask, *"How well are we doing? Are we listening to each other carefully? What is not working in how we deal with each other? How can we improve? Are we excluding ideas or approaches without giving them full consideration?"*

• *Respect for one another and support for one another's ideas.* When the leader is careful to ask questions of, and listen to, every member of the group without exception, it sets a powerful example for everyone on the team. To make sure everyone is included, single out by name those who have held back and ask, *"Do you have anything to add?"*

• *Improved learning and a willingness to help others to learn.* To help members discover how to learn from each other and put that learning to work for the organization's benefit, ask, *"Who has had experience with this issue? Does anyone have a different idea? How do people feel about this in your department?"*

• *A fuller understanding of the situation you are facing.* Gidget Hopf says questions can provide a useful reality check:

My leadership team met after a particularly difficult board meeting, and I went around the table and asked each person: *"What did you hear and what did you come away with from that board meeting?"* This helped us to clarify and validate what we all felt, and it helped me to see how each individual perceived the discussion. We gained a great deal of clarity without its

185

becoming a whining or bitch session. I will also sometimes throw out a thought and ask people to react. For example, with my senior leadership team, I might say the following: *"I am feeling that the team is starting to show some cracks; what are your observations, how do you feel about my observation?"*

Encouraging Open Discussion and Debate

As consultant and author Patrick Lencioni points out, "Teams that fail to disagree and exchange unfiltered opinions . . . find themselves revisiting the same issues again and again."[6] Teams that cannot openly debate and disagree cannot learn effectively, and so they keep going back over the same ground. Adds Lencioni, "CEOs who go to great lengths to avoid conflict often do so believing that they are strengthening their teams by avoiding destructive disagreement. This is ironic, because what they are really doing is stifling productive conflict and pushing important issues that need to be resolved under the carpet, where they will fester." Lencioni stresses that people can feel confident about making a decision with the full benefit of the collective wisdom of the group only after team members have passionately and fully debated with one another.

John Stuart Mill reinforces the importance of vigorous debate in his classic book *On Liberty*, noting the following benefits of hearing the other side of an issue:

> Though the silenced opinion may be in error, it may and very commonly does, contain a portion of truth. It is only by the collision of adverse opinions that the remainder of the truth has any chance of being supplied.

186

Even if the received opinion is not true, the whole truth, unless it is vigorously and earnestly contested, will, by most of those who receive it, be held in the manner of a prejudice, with little comprehension or feeling of its rational grounds. Unless widely held beliefs are challenged by differing opinions, their value is lost.[7]

Asking what others think enhances their participation in whatever decision will ultimately be determined, and consequently increases support for the decision and reduces the risk that the decision might be undermined by either inadequate consideration or unexpected opposition. According to Axelrod, Axelrod, Beedon, and Jacobs, "Meetings require conversations where people can voice their support *and* their doubts. My ability to say yes is only as good as my ability to say no."[8] When the leader uses questions to encourage a full and open debate, doubts can be addressed and resolved. People can come to agree and commit to a course of action, rather than just acquiescing in it. Accountability is the willingness to act in service of the whole; it comes from acts of consent, not acts of mandate or direction. Commitment is the choice to act as an owner. Community is the consciousness that we all have a stake in each other's success. It is our interconnectedness. When we want to ensure we have everyone's wisdom, everyone's point of view, and everyone's commitment, skillful questioning is essential.

I discussed the power of reflection in Chapter 7. Significant learning occurs as a result of getting the group to reflect, and significant reflection occurs as a result of good questions and debate. Through the use of questions, leaders can help group members examine their actions and interactions and thereby

187

improve the quality of debate and of learning, thinking, and creativity. The leader's questions should be open-ended and supportive of diverse points of view. Leaders need to model the listening and questioning skills discussed in Chapter 5. Ask questions that enable the group to air disagreements and to reflect on how they are doing as a group, how they can improve, what they are learning, and how their learning can be applied to themselves and to their organization. Your enthusiasm for learning and your commitment to helping the group succeed should be evident to the group.

Energizing Team Meetings

As noted at the outset of this chapter, team meetings too often sap energy and enthusiasm. When you find people sitting around the table looking bored or distracted, get them engaged by asking questions. Remember Chad Holliday's comment: "I find that when someone engages me in a question, it wakes me up. I'm in a different place." Questions, especially challenging ones, cause the group and the individuals to think and to learn. Questions create energy and vitality in the group by triggering the need to listen, to seek a common truth, to justify opinions and viewpoints. Questions generate a dialogue in which everyone begins to leave their individual limitations to find a new wholeness.

Of course, the way meetings begin often sets the tone for how they proceed and what will be accomplished. Thus questions can get staff meetings off to a good start. Wheatley suggests some of the following questions:

188

- What are procedures that will bring us together?
- How can we listen for what is different (rather than start with fighting)?
- How can our working together be more relaxing and less stressful?[9]

Axelrod and colleagues suggest several ways to use questions to engage people and generate energy during a team meeting:

- Instead of selling your idea, ask meeting participants to identify why your idea won't work. Then listen carefully to what people say. This legitimizes the sharing of doubts and shifts the process from selling to co-creation.
- Give everyone a chance to speak by going around the room and asking where people stand on an issue. Many times conversations are dominated by one or two people. Hearing from everyone often shifts the conversation and allows you to bring closure to an issue.
- Separate understanding from agreement. Simply understanding someone's point of view does not mean agreeing with it, but it builds a bridge. Working for understanding means seeing the world through the other person's eyes. When you do this, you build trust and rapport with that person, and solutions become possible where none existed before.[10]

At the conclusion of the meeting, additional questions should be asked to determine what went well at the meeting as well as what could be improved at the next meeting. Unless you encourage and enable the members to reflect on the just-concluded meeting by asking a few questions, little or no learning or improvement will occur—and your meetings will never get any better. At the end of each session, help the group learn by asking some of the following questions:

- How well has this session gone?
- What has the group done well?
- What could the group do better?
- What are we not doing that we could be doing?
- What actions are we going to take as a group next time that will improve our performance?

Also, when you encourage everyone to focus more on questioning and less on statements, everyone more easily becomes involved in the discussions. One person is less able to dominate. Questions during the meeting also cause individuals and teams to be more receptive to adapting, changing, and growing.

Helping the Team Overcome Obstacles

At any stage of the problem-solving process, a team can get stuck, not seeing a way forward. When a team gets stuck, the members often wait for the positional leader to make a statement, define a problem, or propose a solution. Team members hold back, waiting for the leader to accept responsibility. The wise leader will not fall into this trap. The use of questions is an effective way to keep responsibility where it belongs, as Sue Whitt demonstrated with her team: "When projects were off track, I asked them to think of times they made that choice and why. This got them thinking and speaking. I would ask, 'Why did you take this path? How does this connect to the goals set?'" Whitt's questions prodded her team to accept responsibility for grappling with issues.

To help shake things up so that the team can see things from a new perspective and move forward, it's useful to ask the following types of questions:

- *Open-ended questions*: Unlike closed questions, which seek a short, specific response like yes or no, open-ended questions encourage people to expand ideas and allow exploration of what's important to them or what is comfortable for them to reveal. Asking open-ended questions also encourages them to do the work of self-reflection and problem solving rather than justifying or defending a position. For example: *What do you think about . . . ? Could you say more about . . . ? What possibilities come to mind? What might happen if you . . . ?*

- *Clarification questions*: When someone is not clear or you do not experience a full understanding of a situation, you might ask the person to define or explain the statement. For example: *"Let me see if I am clear. Are you talking about . . . ? Are you saying . . . ? Could you say that in different words?"*

- *Questions for details*: When someone is not clear, you may ask for further bits of information. For example: *"More specifically, what are some of the things that you have tried? Have you asked so-and-so what his major concerns are? Does thus-and-such agree that there are performance problems?"*

- *Stimulating questions*: Introduce ideas and options by asking questions rather than suggesting a course of action. Emphasis is on asking, rather than telling, inviting a thoughtful response and maintaining a spirit of collaboration. For example: "*Let me see if I am clear. Are you talking about setting goals based upon your feedback?*" This implies that person should use feedback as a guide to setting goals. Similarly, "*Have you asked so-and-so what his concerns are?*" can be used to offer someone the option of inviting so-and-so to speak about his priorities.

- *Probing questions*: Go below the level of events and behaviors to search for internal drivers that trigger a person's behavior. For example: "*Why did this happen? Why did you believe this would be the result?*"

- *Summarizing questions*: Invite others to complete or end the discussion with questions that capture the key issues or action. For example: "*What is the major point that has been made here?*"

Charles Ostland, principal of Oakton High School in Oakton, Virginia, describes his approach with teachers who seem stuck: "My favorite question to ask teachers who are dealing with an unsuccessful student is, 'What did you do next, or what else did you try, or . . . and then what?' Although this approach can be annoying at times, it suggests that we are always along some point of a continuum of possibilities and whether we choose to move further along the continuum is, in fact, a choice, often limited only by the questions we choose to ask."

Although Ostland is talking about helping individuals get unstuck, his approach applies equally well with teams. Whether we allow ourselves to become stuck is, as he says, a choice.

QUESTIONS HELP YOU MANAGE TEAM CONFLICT

Conflict over ideas is natural, healthy, and to be expected, as teams are organized so as to gain benefits of multiple perspectives. Conflict is an integral part of the team process. Team members with multiple perspectives will inevitably view issues differently and should seek to learn from each other in the process of resolving these differences. Healthy conflict is focused on task issues over which there may be legitimate differences of opinion, or differences in values and perspectives, or expectations about the impact of decisions.[11] Questions are the mode of healthy group conflict.

Conflict becomes unhealthy when it involves competition over power, rewards, and resources; when communications are faulty or personal grudges intervene; when team meetings are poorly run; or when individuals seek to make individual goals take precedence over group goals. Statements are the common communication mode of unhealthy conflict.

What are some questions that a leader can employ when managing team conflicts? How can we develop trust and rapport among the participants? Ury suggests the following questions:

1. How can we separate the people from the problem— diagnose the cause of the conflict?

2. What goals are in conflict?

3. What does each side want?

4. Do all sides have a clear understanding of the issues?

5. How can I encourage them to view the conflict from the other side's perspective and to practice active listening?

6. What are the common areas of interest?

7. What are the issues (not What is each side's position)?

8. How can each side get what it wants?

9. What are the issues that are incompatible between the two sides?

10. What are the most important goals of each side?

11. How can we generate options that can be used to solve the problem?

12. What objective criteria will we use as a basis for our decisions?

13. How can we disagree in an agreeable fashion?[12]

Eric Charoux is a partner at De Chazal Du Mee and executive director of DCDM Business School in Mauritius. He provides an insightful analysis of the power of questions in dealing with conflict. "Asking questions," he told me, "transforms conflict into confusion." When we focus rigidly on our own point of view, we cannot see another's. Questions about our point of view can confuse us, and in that state, we become open to looking at other possibilities. When the team as a whole becomes confused, it is ripe for exploring new possibilities.

Jayan Warrier, director of Latitude Leadership, described to me how a question enabled a group he was leading to move from conflict to learning.

Once I was responsible for managing a planning session with a high-potential team of ten members. Initially, the session was running smoothly, with the team identifying strategic objectives, key goals, and measurable success criteria. Suddenly, at some point, the team divided into two and conflicts began to emerge. Debates escalated into arguments, with some members shutting down and others pushing aggressively. After twenty minutes, I intervened with the question, "What specific point in time did you stop working together as a team?" As team members reflected and turned the flip chart pages back, they realized that they had prematurely divided themselves into task groups and assigned tasks before major team decisions were made. This realization was a major turning point in the team, and was a lesson that guided them for their remaining days as a team.

Questions asked among group members provide a number of benefits to the team: Questions build trust, collaboration, and cohesion among team members. They assist us in clarifying and reaching consensus on goals and actions. Questions help members at different levels of authority and expertise to provide valuable contributions. And only through questioning each other can a group gain a common understanding of and agreement on the problem, acquire a sense of each other's potential strategies, and achieve innovative strategies. In short, questions asked at the right time and in the right way provide the glue that brings and holds a group together.

SHARING RESPONSIBILITY

As noted in Chapter 2, when we ask questions of others and invite them to search for answers with us, we are not just sharing information; we are also sharing responsibility. Teams are all about sharing responsibility. While a traditional leader may see a team as merely a convenient vehicle for command and control and may withhold information and responsibility, the leaders I have interviewed know that this is no longer effective in today's world. Teams function best when responsibility is shared, ideas are shared, problems are shared, and ownership for results is shared. Helping everyone on the team become a better questioner is thus an important way to improve teamwork.

QUESTIONS FOR REFLECTION

1. What are questions that I could use to facilitate or coach rather than control teams?
2. How can I encourage initiative and risk taking?
3. How do I collaborate with team members?
4. How can I better lead my teams with questions?
5. How do I get team members to have different perspectives?
6. How do I encourage open discussions and dialogue in team meetings?
7. How can I energize my team meetings?

8. What are questions that I can use to effectively handle conflict?
9. How do I get the team members to share responsibility?
10. How can I help my teams ask better questions to solve problems?

Using Questions to Solve Problems

How many times have you jumped straight into the solutions to a problem, only to realize later that, if you had first asked questions and listened, you could have come up with much better answers. Nilofer Merchant notes that problem solving is all about smart(er) questions. Smart questions can "define the problem well and lead to a clear vision of the issues involved."[1] Gaining clarity about the problem makes it easier and more likely that you will arrive at actions that are powerful and sustainable.

Frank Andracchi of the Constellation Generation Group stresses the importance of questions whenever he is involved in problem solving: "Using questions to solve problems, explore issues, and minimize the influence of different personalities during the problem-solving process is extremely powerful." For one problem-solving session with his team, the group agreed to the ground rule (from Action Learning, a training program described in Resource B) that team members could make statements only in response to questions. As a result, he says, "I found the use of questions resulted in a clear definition of the problem and a much more open flow of information, as the group could only answer the questions, and by focusing on asking and answering questions, a significant improvement in comprehension of the information presented. I quickly realized that the use of the right questions was a better leadership tool than the traditional trading of statements."

Leaders should deliberately seek a variety of perspectives in solving problems—and the more complex the problem, the more important it is to seek diversity of perspectives. Even though they create some challenges at first, these different initial perspectives are positive and valuable for problem solving and strategy development. Why? For one thing, as I noted in Chapter 2, we generally assume that, having heard about or experienced the problem, we now know and understand exactly what the problem is. And, even more dangerously, we believe everyone else now has the same perception and understanding of the problem. But different people who hear about or even experience the same problem will in fact discern it and describe it quite differently. This is especially true when we face adaptive problems.

TECHNICAL AND ADAPTIVE PROBLEMS

Heifetz and Laurie describe two types of problems faced by organizations and leaders today.[2] *Technical problems* are those in which the necessary knowledge to solve the problem already

200

exists in a documented form or set of procedures. Solving these problems requires the acquisition and application of knowledge in an efficient and rational way, applied in what can be described as a Newtonian manner. Technical problems have a linear, logical solution, with precedents within or outside the organization; they are puzzles with single right answers. Technical problems are somewhat mechanical and may require few if any questions, particularly great questions. *Adaptive problems*, however, are problems for which no satisfactory response has yet been developed and no technical expertise is fully adequate. Questions, reflection, and learning are required both to define the problem and to implement solutions. The challenge of the leader in these types of problems is to mobilize people to make painful adjustments in their attitudes, work habits, basic assumptions, and other aspects of their lives, while at the same time learning their way into the creation of something that does not yet exist.

Adaptive problems have no ready solutions. They require people to apply their collective intelligence and individual skills to the work that only they can do. Meeting this responsibility requires unlearning the habits of a managerial lifetime, new learning to meet challenges for which current skills are insufficient, and capacity to explore and understand the competing values at stake. Adaptive problems are more difficult to define and resolve precisely than technical problems, because they require efforts of people throughout the organization.

Adaptive work is frequently avoided—and the avoidance mechanisms are often unconscious. Reality testing is often an early victim of disequilibrium. Initially, people will apply routine practices for realistically assessing and addressing problems. If these routines do not work, restoring equilibrium may take precedence over the prolonged uncertainty associated with weighing divergent views and facing the need for changing attitudes and beliefs.

GAINING AN UNDERSTANDING OF THE REAL PROBLEM THROUGH QUESTIONS

Dolphins use a form of sonar to "see" in murky or dark water, using a click sound and waiting for the echo to return. Once they have a sufficient number of echo responses, they can navigate and find their food, as well as avoid obstacles and predators. Merchant observes that "questions are the business equivalent of sonar. Asking the right questions can assist you in finding the right, the real problem. Questions can also act as a filter to decipher the key issues in the situation."[3]

Questions are needed not just to seek answers, but also to motivate everyone involved to seek understanding, to respond to what is being asked, to force us to think. The focus is not on a quest for solutions only but also a quest for opportunities to explore and to learn. For purposes of problem exploration and solving, research shows that questions are always more powerful than statements in clarifying, in gaining mutual agreement, in reaching a consensus of perspective.[4]

Whether we are facing a technical or an adaptive problem, the obvious (but unfortunately uncommon) first step is to be sure the group knows what the problem is. Thus different perspectives and the resulting fresh questions become critical for a full understanding of the problem (for example, that it is an elephant), and only when there is agreement that it is indeed an elephant can workable strategies emerge that will enable us to move the elephant (for example, tapping the elephant's side or offering a treat). The acquisition of a wide, panoramic view of the problem can be accomplished only by openly and freshly questioning each other and then reflecting on the responses.

Effective problem solving requires an environment that allows for and encourages people to ask dumb or, more accurately, *fresh* questions. We should focus on generating questions and look for the right questions to start with, rather than jumping directly to finding right answers. The right questions will lead us to right answers. Questions help everyone in the group recognize and reorganize their knowledge. As group members are engaged in asking questions of each other, they gradually gain a group consensus on answers and strategies, as they now more clearly see one another's perspectives as well as gaining a greater clarity of their own.

When Warner-Lambert was acquired by Pfizer, Robert Hoffman was one of four people chosen in Ann Arbor to provide full-time support to the integration activities. These activities were widely seen as best practice and were documented extensively in the press and academic literature. Hoffman found that the use of questions showed that one problem they were dealing with was not located where they thought it was, in the technical issues of drug development:

"On one project I identified data that suggested we were not as efficient in drug development process as we needed to be. I asked questions relative to possible causes with other people. We determined, through a series of questions, that the problem was poor team leadership. Questions changed our entire way of selecting people for team leadership role. Pfizer accepted it totally. In the past, our leaders were good scientists and chemists but not leaders. As a result of our questions, we developed a new competency model."

Through questions, the group carefully determines whether solving the original problem really resolves the situation. Gaining clarity and consensus on the real problem is thus the first and most important part of problem solving, for if we jump for solutions too soon, we may end up solving the wrong problem. Designing a new drug development process would not have helped Hoffman.

QUESTIONS AS THE ESSENCE FOR BREAKTHROUGH PROBLEM SOLVING

Great thinkers who change the world create their own questions, becoming their "own Socrates," as Burger and Starbird put it in their bestselling *The 5 Elements of Effective Thinking*.[5] Creating questions is as important as answering them, enlivening your curiosity so that you are much better at problem solving. Asking questions can reveal hidden assumptions and enable a problem solver or problem-solving team to become better at considering alternatives.

Jean-Paul Gaillard says that questions have enabled him to achieve some marvelous successes in his years as a senior executive with companies such as Movenpick, Warner Electric, Phillip Morris, and Nestlé. He told me how his questions enabled the Bertucci Watch Company to match and even exceed the quality of the Rolex brand.

> I use questions to get people to aim high and become energized and creative. With the Bertucci watch, I challenged workers that caused them to surpass their current strategies. How can we become smarter? How can we take advantage of our smaller size? Are we sure that this is all we can do? What are our strengths? Is there a better way? The result was a great watch, with 20 percent more quality than a Rolex, a firm and more comfortable band, and at a much lower price.

Shamir Ally, a global consultant and financial advisor, has found questions to be critical in his work with organizations around the world. While working in Guyana, Shamir was a member of a team tasked with the responsibility of preparing an action plan for the economic transformation of the country. "I posed the question, 'What can the government of Guyana do to attract foreign investors?'" This simple but direct question led to a number of changes in how the government promoted the country, including a focus on English fluency, culture, and natural resources. In Qatar, Shamir, while working with the University's School of Business and Finance, posed the question: "How could all six Gulf countries [Qatar, Saudi Arabia, Kuwait, United Arab Emirates, Bahrain, and Oman] integrate their Enterprise Resource Planning (ERP) systems?" This led to unprecedented levels of collaborative data-sharing and metrics. In Romania, Shamir's question, "What actions are needed to have Romanians use their own wines and agriculture products?" led to a successful "Buy Romanian" campaign in the face of European regulations limiting exports.

QUESTIONS AT VARIOUS STAGES OF PROBLEM SOLVING

Daudelin points out how questions can and should be asked at each stage of the problem-solving process to obtain information, stimulate reflection, develop insights, and apply knowledge and learning to future actions.[6] Questions are used to open up possibilities, to clarify meaning, and to structure the progression through the four stages of problem solving. Specifically, she identifies particular types of questions that may be most beneficial at each stage of the problem-solving process:

• *Problem articulation and reframing: What* questions are best at this stage; they allow the group to gather details and descriptions of the situation and help members understand the real problem and thus reframe it in a way that everyone can agree on. For example, "*What* is the most import thing . . . ?"

• *Problem analysis stage*: At this stage, *why* questions are most helpful; questions such as "*Why* is that important? *Why* do you think it happened? *Why* were you feeling that way?"

• *Hypothesis generation or diagnosis stage: How* questions allow the group or individual to begin to formulate a tentative theory to explain or address the problem: "*How* is this situation similar to or different from other problems? *How* might you do things differently? *How* could we intervene?"

• *Action stage*: At this stage, the group may be seeking to describe behavior (test for different behaviors) or to share inferences (test for different views); *what* questions become important again. "*What* are the implications of all this for future action? *What* should you do now?"

206

Bianco-Mathis and colleagues present a slightly different model of the problem-solving process, as shown in Exhibit 9.1.[7] Their model also includes suggested questions for different stages.

Exhibit 9.1. Questioning via Dialogue

What to Do	Questions to Ask
State your assumptions: "Here's what I think, and here's how I got there."	
Ask for input.	Do you have different information?
Encourage different points of view.	Does anyone see it differently? How else could we look at this? What other options could we consider?
Explore others' reasoning.	What leads you to think that? What factor contributes to that conclusion?
Invite them to present their data.	Can you walk me through that so I can see how you got there?
Check your understanding.	Am I correct that you're saying . . . ? Does this mean that you would like to see . . . ?
Link their view and yours.	
Identify a larger context or meaning.	How will this affect our stated commitment to preferred vendors? Can you describe how this might look to our customers?

(continued)

Exhibit 9.1 (*continued*)

What to Do	Questions to Ask
Work for agreement on steps.	What can we build on to meet our objective? How can we use what we've identified to achieve our goal? What can we do next to move this forward?

Source: Adapted from Bianco-Mathis et al. (2002), p. 71.

As teams go through the problem-solving process, questions can help them move from one stage to the next. Robert Hoffman explains how he uses questions for this purpose:

"In a research-based organization like Novartis, our people are outside the norm in terms of raising questions at meetings; they are more prone to be investigative, and it is more difficult to gain closure and integration. I have discovered that the best way to reach closure and consolidate our thinking is to ask questions and to check out what I have heard. *'This is what it sounds like; am I correct? What are the options? What should we choose?'*"

Only through questions can a group truly gain a common understanding of the problem, acquire a sense of each other's potential strategies, and achieve innovative breakthrough strategies and solutions. Questions, when asked at the right time in the right way, provide the glue that holds the group together. The seeds of the answer are contained in the kernel of the questions. Thus the better the questions, the better will be the solutions as well as the learning; the deeper the reflections, the greater the development of individual and team competencies.

By beginning with questions, we recognize that problem solving must begin by first diverging through the use of inquiry; only then should the converging and narrowing occur. It is first necessary for a group to gain the big picture of the problem, to "see the entire elephant," before determining possible goals and specific strategies. The acquisition of a wide "helicopter view" of the problem can be accomplished only by openly and freshly questioning each other and then reflecting on the responses. A central aspect of action learning is the reflective inquiry process and the resulting group environment that allows for and encourages people to ask dumb or, more accurately, fresh questions.

The ability to ask good questions is essential in challenging various perspectives that open potential pathways for creative problem solving. When the problem owner asks learning questions, it creates a different energy and dynamism in the group. Learning questions are open-ended *what if*, *how*, and *why* questions to jolt the minds of problem solvers into understanding many other possible scenarios through which the problem at hand could present itself.

Deep questioning of assumptions and ambiguities helps group members gain greater balance in the way they prioritize their actions and at the same time prepares them psychologically for the lessons to be learned. Group members begin to realize that learning and action are equally important and necessary for their development as leaders rather than problem solvers. Once they realize this, the group will have a deeper level of engagement to help them go beyond problem solving to gaining new insights about their learning ability.

As members reflect on the key issues and challenges as a result of their collaborative experience, they begin to formulate new frames of references for subsequent action taking. Such a mental process involves a series of unlearning and relearning to help them develop their new course of action. The intrinsic benefits of questions and reflection must be supported by the right mindset, value, and attitude of the action learning members. Without the right motivation, it will be a challenge for individuals to translate learning into proper action.

WHAT ENABLES A GROUP TO ASK QUESTIONS WHEN SOLVING PROBLEMS?

Roland Yeo and I, in our study of successful problem-solving groups, identified five essential attributes that contribute to effectiveness and innovation:

1. *Thoughtful questioning.* For groups to be effective in solving problems, they must be able to ask useful, systemic, and insightful questions. Asking the right questions enables the group to see things in the appropriate perspective and solve the problem at hand in a much more concerted and thoughtful way.

2. *Self-directedness.* It is important that individual participants possess an intrinsic motivation to undertake learning as a continuous pursuit of personal and professional

improvement. They must take responsibility for their learning to enhance their self-efficacy in their action-taking.

3. *Learning orientation.* Learning from other members while working within the group is a crucial aspect of enlarging worldviews and building on each other's experiences. Learning thereby becomes valuable in developing good, if not great questions.

4. *Deep listening.* For a group to come up with great questions, all members need to be keen observers and listeners during the problem-solving process. Reflective listening helps to remove doubts and provide the cognitive capacity for participants to analyze things more clearly.

5. *Confidence and well-being.* All participants should feel that they have something important to contribute to the action-learning process. Group members should support and encourage each other to ask questions. This will allow them to better deal with doubts and ambiguity, and thereby have the strength to work through difficult issues and develop great strategies.[8]

IMPROVING QUESTIONS WHILE PROBLEM SOLVING

Perhaps the greatest and most critical skill in problem solving is the ability of the individual or the group to improve their questions while they are in the actual problem-solving situation. Taking a few moments to reflect on the questions being asked can lead to even greater problem-solving questions. Thus we could ask ourselves some of the following questions:

211

- What is the quality of our questions?
- What types of questions are being asked?
- Are we building on each other's questions?
- Have any questions been most valuable?
- How can we improve on our questions?
- What has been the impact of our questions?

The better our questions, the better will be our ability to understand and solve problems.

QUESTIONS FOR REFLECTION

1. Am I focusing on questions rather than answers when solving problems?
2. How can I determine whether it is a technical or adaptive problem?
3. Do I use different types of questions for different stages of problem solving?
4. Do I reflect on what has been already asked and learned before asking the next question?
5. Do I frame questions with a curious and breaking-new-ground attitude?
6. Do I look for root causes and seek to solve problems with systems thinking?
7. Do I ask fresh questions to develop fresh perspectives and challenge assumptions?
8. Do I explore potential issues embedded in each question asked?
9. How can I build shared understanding of the problem?
10. How can I generate more creative alternatives, actions, and strategies with my questions?

Using Questions to Shape Strategy and Enable Change

When leaders shape corporate vision, purpose, and strategy, their focus must turn outward, and the questions they ask must go far beyond the company's walls. Questions involving corporate strategy are questions about how the organization relates to the world around it: what markets it competes in, what customers it serves, what alliances it pursues with partners, how it produces its products and services and outsources work to vendors, and how it relates to the community and other stakeholders. Vision and values also must look outward—for although we cannot look to others to tell us what our values should be, our values must be informed by the perspectives of outside stakeholders and relevant to the challenges we face. In this chapter, I explore ways to use questions to shape strategy and promote change, focusing on questions with both internal and external stakeholder groups.

USING QUESTIONS TO BRING FRESH PERSPECTIVE

People can easily become entrapped in the organization's accumulated knowledge and established procedures. As leaders, we must periodically question the collective wisdom of the organization. We need to be able to question assumptions about structures, strategies, values, and business processes that shape the organization's culture and operations. In addressing strategic issues, a fresh perspective is absolutely essential if the organization is to perceive new opportunities, uncover hidden and potentially threatening trends in the marketplace, and create new business models.

As Adams noted, "Asking questions is essential for opening new possibilities for virtually every goal and function, whether it's gathering information, building relationships, thinking objectively, coordinating supply chain activities. Skillful questioning is also fundamental for resolving breakdowns, making tough decisions, innovating, and managing change."[1]

When Kevin Sharer became CEO of Amgen, he interviewed the top hundred executives at the company, even though he'd already been president for eight years. "Whether or not you are new to the company, you have to bring a new set of eyes," he told the *Wall Street Journal*. He asked each executive these five questions:

- What do you want to keep?
- What do you want to change?
- What do you want me to do?
- What are you afraid I'll do?
- What else do you want to ask me?[2]

214

Together, Sharer and his top executives agreed to a new vision for the company, to make Amgen "the best therapeutic company" as it expanded its market beyond dialysis to more competitive drug markets.

Questions can open up new possibilities for virtually every organizational goal and function, be it the understanding of emerging markets, the gathering of information, the building of key relationships, thinking objectively, learning, or developing an organization. Deep questions about structures, strategies, and values function as openhanded invitations to creativity, calling forth that which doesn't yet exist. Thus, as Adams noted in a recent conversation with me: "The springboard to every discovery can be understood as the right question, asked at the right time, in the right way, and to the right person(s)."

Walt Disney World (WDW) discovered the power of questions when dealing with an 85 percent employee turnover rate at their laundry services. Initially Disney considered outsourcing laundry to another company. However, when their leadership met, they decided to try another approach and to push the decision down to the cast members (all employees at WDW are called cast members). The cast members were asked two questions:

1. What can we do to make your job easier?
2. What changes would you recommend to serve our guests better?

Initially cast members did not feel the freedom to share their thoughts, fearing that their responses would be viewed as criticism. It took about six months of asking before the cast members began to engage. But when the cast members began to share their ideas, Disney leaders listened, and changes were made. Based on the suggestions of the cast members, today all cast members can raise or lower the platform on which they are standing to an ideal working height. In addition, air conditioning vents are now directly overhead in their work areas. They had been using a hook-type tool to empty the dirty laundry carts, which was tearing a lot of bedsheets. Engineering was brought in, and with the cast members' help, the engineers redesigned this tool, saving several hundred thousand dollars a year. Other changes included redesigning the machine that automatically folds sheets and towels. The machine has bands that move the sheets and towels forward, but there was a problem—the bands quite often broke, stopping the whole process. One of the cast members who had recently left the Navy had an idea. He had learned to tie a special knot in the Navy that he thought could be used to tie together the ends of a broken band. It worked, with an annual cost savings to Disney of over $100,000![3]

Questions about strategy, vision, and values should be treated not as technical problems, but as adaptive problems, as discussed in Chapter 9. In dealing with adaptive problems, we need to provide a forum for active debate and drive the organization to find new questions rather than easy answers. We do this by developing a questioning culture throughout the organization, as described in Chapter 6. To recap briefly, leaders must be willing to say "*I don't know*" and model the frequent use of questions. We need to encourage everyone in the organization to challenge the status quo, take risks, and ask more questions—and to reward those who do. Offer training on effective questioning, problem solving, and teamwork to back up exhortation with resources and action.

Peter and Lily Cheng, codirectors of PACE OD, have assisted hundreds of organizations throughout Asia and Europe in transformations. They shared with me the questions they recommend that leaders use for moving from the current situation to their desired future:

1. Questions to encourage the organization to take action
   - What is the compelling vision that would create an urgency for change?
   - How do we inspire others to achieve remarkable things?
   - What evidence can we not afford to ignore to warrant a change?
   - How can we shake others out of their comfort zone?
   - What structure, systems, and processes must be in place to drive the change?
2. Questions to transition the change
   - What are the easy steps to begin to set a positive momentum for the change to get going?
   - How can we involve others in change ownership? What roles should people play in the change initiative?
   - How can we allow others to air their concerns in the process of change?
   - What kind of competencies would be necessary for people to change effectively?

- What structure must be in place to facilitate behavioral change?

3. Questions to sustain the new change
   - What should be done to ensure there is no way back to the old equilibrium?
   - How can we institutionalize the change into the formal systems and structures?
   - What can we do to ensure that people continue to look into the future?
   - What reward would be necessary to sustain the desired behaviors?

QUESTIONING STAKEHOLDERS OUTSIDE THE ORGANIZATION

The importance of questioning people outside the organization has continued to grow as companies become ever more dependent on such partners both inside and outside the business chain for information, business, resources, and collaboration. The demarcations between management and employees, between departments and units, between employees and customers, between the company and its vendors, and even between the company and its competitors have become less permanent and more flexible.

Empowering and enabling these various groups of people through questions extends and strengthens the organization. Asking questions outside the organization and outside one's culture may be a difficult challenge for a leader; however, such questions not only cannot be avoided, they must be welcomed, as the responses they acquire from outsiders may serve as the key and impetus of a leader's ultimate success.

Leaders at all levels, including senior leaders, need to create opportunities for asking questions of individuals and groups outside the organization—customers, business partners, suppliers, community groups, and academic and training institutions. Questioning such groups is often vital to the long-term success of the enterprise. Several years ago, Michael Hammer chronicled a number of corporate successes and failures that had occurred in the global marketplace.[4] He examined why Wal-Mart overcame Sears; why Pan Am, the leading global airline of the mid-twentieth century, ceased to exist; and why Howard Johnson was beaten by McDonald's, Burger King, and KFC. All these failures, he concluded, shared one underlying cause—leadership did not ask the probing questions that might have led them to challenge their basic assumptions, to refresh their strategies, and to fundamentally change their ways of operating. Such questions might have prevented the decline or death of these companies.

Peter Drucker says that in shaping our organizations for the future, we must look at society and community by asking these questions:

> What changes have already happened that do not fit "what everybody knows"? What are the "paradigm changes"? Is there any evidence that this is a change and not a fad? And finally, one then asks, "If this change is relevant and meaningful, what opportunities does it offer?"[5]

Questions for Customers

Many companies recognize the importance of corporate leadership's asking questions of their customers. Senior executives of Motorola, including the CEO, meet personally and regularly with customers to ask about the company's services and products. Worthington Steel machine operators make periodic trips to customers' factories to discover their needs via questions. They actively seek feedback, suggestions, and consultation with customers and suppliers.

Canadian Imperial Bank of Commerce (CIBC) is very familiar with the critical importance of learning about their customers through ongoing questions. The bank and everyone in it recognize that they need to know more about the customers and their individually evolving needs. For business customers, it means understanding their industry and their strategy and agenda, and providing solutions to their problems rather than selling previously defined products and services. The process works both ways; customers also need to know more about what banks can provide. For example, derivatives are a complex and valuable set of risk management tools, but often not well understood, even by sophisticated corporate finance managers.

Although asking questions of customers is of course useful for finding out how your company is currently doing with them, an even greater benefit can be derived from using questions to create the future together. Rather than focusing just on how current products and services are meeting customer needs, effective leaders focus on the customers' goals and aspirations. Douglas Eden, president of Cargill's Malt Americas unit, explained to me how he does this:

> I use questions to explore, discover, and create solutions. We wish to be seen as a solutions company which is able to create meaningful value to ourselves and to others. Asking questions of the customers is more powerful for Cargill than selling what Cargill does. As a result, we have systematically built questions into our conversations with customers, questions such as: "What are your goals? What is holding you back from achieving these goals? What are consequences of not achieving your goals? What have you tried to overcome these obstacles? How much is the problem costing the business? In your opinion, what would be the ideal solution for the issue?"
>
> When I first began leading at Malt Americas, we were a business that was losing money. I needed people who were willing to take risks, had self-confidence, and were ready to buy into a new vision. Now, four years later, we are a successful business. I attribute much of this success to our ability to ask questions—and to our customers, who were willing to answer our questions. Our business is very complex, and we have to search for the answers together.

By focusing on customer *needs*, Eden was able to turn around a faltering enterprise. And by focusing on customer *goals*, Eden is able to go beyond improving today's business to building tomorrow's. Of course, that is a large part of what strategy is all about.

Customers will increasingly determine how organizations set strategies and carry out operations. Customers rather than workers will become the focus of leadership attention and organizational priorities. On a worldwide scale, customers will continue to push for new performance standards in quality, variety, customization, convenience, time saving, and innovation. Top leadership at Milliken, a large textile and chemical manufacturing company located in Spartanburg, South Carolina, clearly recognize the importance of questions in encouraging and supporting the customer's expectations of improved quality, new innovations, and quicker speed. Milliken staff, for example, accompany the first shipment of each of the company's products to see how it is used and exploit these opportunities to ask questions aimed at finding further product improvements.

Jeanette Partlow, president of Maryland Chemical Company, recognizes the importance of using questions in reaching customers and shaping strategy:

"My company, my coworkers, and I use questions to deliver absolute customer satisfaction and build customers for life. In pursuit of this mission … we use questions to conduct customer, supplier, employee, market, and economic assessments that we use in our business and strategic planning. We use questions to problem solve and troubleshoot. We use questions to innovate."

In 78 *Important Questions Every Leader Should Ask and Answer*, Clarke-Epstein has identified several questions that she considers the most critical to ask customers:

- Why do you do business with us?
- Why do you do business with our competitors?

- How and when have we made it hard for you to do business with us?
- What will you need from us in the future?
- If you were me, what's one thing you'd change about my organization?
- What's the most effective way to tell you that we are grateful for your business?
- Suppose this organization could choose just three things to do more or differently to dramatically enhance our customers' loyalty—what would they be?[6]

Leeds notes that working in the sales field requires a series of questions designed to uncover needs and wants, to build relationships, and to foster commitment.[7] Thriving organizations create and maintain exceptional levels of customer loyalty. Loyal customers are great customers. Loyalty, however, is something we must earn. How do we get such loyalty? The best way, according to Bell and Bell, is by asking questions and listening to what our customers want and, whenever possible, exceeding their expectations.[8]

Research shows that successful salespeople ask up to 58 percent more questions than unsuccessful ones do. Employees on the front lines, be it in sales or service, realize that they can succeed only to the extent that they have knowledge about the marketplace. And their most important knowledge about the individual customer can come only from the questions they ask those customers. Conversations and information gathering from customers provide up-to-date product information, competitive comparisons, insights into changing preferences, and immediate feedback about service and patterns of use.

Questions for Vendors and Partners

The growing presence of global competition and virtual organizations has drastically increased the number of short-term alliances formed between and among companies. Most companies use alliances for the purpose of increasing profits and market share as well as for cutting expenses, time, duplication, and politics. Inquiring leaders, however, seek to add another very important, long-term benefit to the alliance—learning.

Perceptive leaders quickly realize that their success depends heavily on the success of the company's entire business network, not just its employees and customers but also its suppliers, vendors, and partners. Manville notes how organizations need to embrace the extended enterprise.[9] Organizations have become more virtual through such mechanisms as outsourcing, core competency focus, and the host of alliances, joint ventures, and partnerships affiliated with every company. People—be they employees, contractors, partners, or suppliers—must now work together in value chains to deliver the needed goods and services to customers. Although the links among the pieces of the chain are contractual, they are also defined by exchanges of knowledge, values, and other intangibles.

Questioning (and learning from) partners and vendors has become a critical process across all types of organizations today. Having others in the business chain collectively learn about commitments and policies as well as appropriate management or technical skills can be very valuable to everyone's long-range fortunes. Resources available from vendors and partners, including the gaining of intelligence and competencies via questions, can be critical for the survival of the company. They can also provide competitive advantage.

"Questions are very valuable with technical suppliers and software vendors at Pfizer," Sue Whitt says. "We needed to be and were leading-edge by design and were willing to pay the price for what would provide competitive advantage. My questions with vendors and suppliers were more direct: 'Why are you not doing what we requested? How can we make this work? What can make this faster? How can we get better consultants? How are we going to get it *done?*'"

According to Booz Allen Hamilton consultants John R. Harbison and Peter Pekar Jr., companies that are successful alliance builders "reach out for knowledge and expertise.... They know from experience that learning counts—and counts big. They set up systems and processes to transfer alliance learning and experience to key managers and hold training sessions and workshops. They also create repositories of knowledge to be tapped into." Harbison and Pekar cite Oracle, Xerox, IBM, Hewlett-Packard, Motorola, Merck, and Johnson & Johnson as successful alliance builders, each having formed more than a hundred alliances.

According to Harbison and Pekar:

The important question is no longer, "Should we form a strategic alliance?" Now the questions are:

1. What types of arrangements are most appropriate?
2. How do we successfully manage these alliances?
3. Are we learning from the experience of ourselves and others?[10]

Up front, at the very beginning of the relationship, the leader should consider what learning is possible from the alliance—customer intelligence, process, and operations policies, cultural nuances, and so on. You may even want to build these learning objectives into the agreement. Leaders (and their learning companies) then should provide an adequate exchange of personnel to be sure to capture and bring the learning back. The alliance provides valuable learning and therefore becomes a rich, long-term investment and profit center that can be used as a basis for future successes.

In forming partnerships and alliances, all parties need to come to clear understandings—and asking the right questions is critical to that process. Stuart Kliman, a founding partner of Vantage Partners LLC, a Boston-based consulting group that specializes in relationship management and strategic alliances, has firm views about the proper procedure at the beginning of any partnership, as *Fast Company* reports in "Seven Strategies for Successful Alliances." Kliman elaborates on the third strategy, "To end well, start smart":

> Begin the relationship with a structured launch process.
>
> "Get key people in a room together, and answer these questions: What's our relationship vision? How should we work together to meet our objectives? What challenges will we likely face given our particular business context, the current economic conditions, and our differing strategies?" Kliman says. "Figure out all the challenges that will make it difficult to work together: How are we going to manage conflict? How are we going to handle surprises? How are we going to deal with breakdowns in trust?" Also, determine

226

how those messages will be communicated to the rest of the organization.[11]

Chad Holliday, DuPont's CEO, agrees, saying, "We need to ask all the stakeholders questions—those who supply DuPont, buy from DuPont, sell for DuPont." Companies can share learning with their network in many ways. For example, companies can use certifications to qualify not only their own people but also their partners and suppliers. Ford Motor Company, for example, asks questions and uses the learning from those questions to ensure appropriate procedures, technical expertise, and brand management among its dealerships. Anheuser-Busch asks questions to determine the training needed for distributors in the handling of food and beverage products to maintain quality and brand. Cisco, through its constant questioning, is creating higher customer satisfaction and support for faster product rollout by offering learning programs and tools to its channel partners, who provide 70 percent of revenue. Toyota pioneered the use of questions and learning in qualifying and aligning its suppliers; and the "work with us, learn from us, teach us" principle now governs thousands of manufacturing and supplier relationships around the world.

Questions for the Community

A leader who leads with questions quickly recognizes the many benefits that accrue from involving the community as a part of the questioning chain—benefits such as the enhancement of the company's image in the community, the generation of greater community interest in working for or buying from the company, the strengthening of the quality of life in the community, the preparation of a future workforce, and the opportunity to exchange and share community resources. In addition, in working with local schools, the leader may be able to create a win-win situation; that is, allowing teachers and community leaders to participate in corporate training programs and allowing employees to become tutors or resources for teachers and students in the classroom. The local institutions, in turn, can jointly sponsor learning events with the company.

James Austin of the Harvard Business School says community involvement by business leaders is too often "the invisible side of leadership."[12] This is unfortunate, in that leaders who are visible and accessible to the community and the media can be more effective spokespersons for the organization. Relationships between business, the community, and government are often particularly fragile and can easily fray. Leaders who are out of touch with community sentiment and values often step on toes without even realizing it.

In asking questions of community leaders, we should adapt a learning mindset, with the aim of understanding their values, concerns, goals, and aspirations for the community. These are just some of the questions you should consider asking:

- How do you feel about our company?
- What can we do to help make our relationship with the community better?
- Is there something you think we do that we should stop doing?

- What do you want us to start doing?
- What sort of information would you like us to provide about the company?

Just as important—if not more so—is making yourself available to *answer* questions from the community. People can be suspicious of business, and being reluctant to answer questions openly and forthrightly often reinforces the feeling that you have something to hide. No doubt some questions will be accusatory and others will be designed to promote an agenda. You will still want to try to answer openly and display a learner mindset, as described in Chapter 5. By demonstrating a learner mindset yourself, you can encourage others to move away from a judger mindset.

DEVELOPING STRATEGIC VISION AND VALUES

Once your company has gained a full picture of the current reality by asking questions of all stakeholders, it has the context it needs to begin talking about its vision for the future and the values that will help guide it there. Effective visions are developed through conversations, not lamination. They are motivated by relationships generated through the leaders' questions. Seeds of change and future possibilities are created through the questions that leaders ask.

Questions can also build corporate *values*. Questions are fateful; they create a conversational agenda, which in turn becomes the context for envisioning and enacting the future. The more positive the question, the more positive will be the potential for transformation.

229

What then are some of the questions used by leaders to build corporate vision, purpose, and values? Ken Blanchard, noted author of books such as *The One-Minute Manager, Full Steam Ahead*, and *The Secret: What Great Managers Know—and Do*, has identified five key high-level questions in determining the direction of the organization. First, to determine the *purpose or mission* of the company, the leader should ask, "What business are we in? The *image* or picture of the company can be developed by responding to the question, What will the future look like if things are running as planned? The *values* of the company are determined by the question, What do we stand for?" *Goals* are determined by "What do we want people to focus on now?" Blanchard then emphasizes the asking of the *ethical* question: Is it legal, fair, and not harmful to self-esteem?[13]

Peter Drucker, after studying organizations and leaders for more than fifty years, discovered that the effective leaders he had met, worked with, and observed behaved in a very similar way. They started out by asking, "What needs to be done?" Then they asked, "What can I do and should I do to make a difference?" They constantly asked, "What are the organization's mission and goals? What constitutes performance and results in this organization?" They were not afraid of strength in their associates. They also asked, "What in my organization could I do that would truly make a difference?" and finally, "How can I truly set an example?"[14]

Marilee Goldberg advises leaders to ask some of the following questions when considering organizational vision and strategy:

• What options have we considered [and] not considered?

- How can this be the best possible win-win?
- What limitations might we be placing on thinking, planning, or actions?
- How else can we think about this?
- Are we being honest with ourselves?
- What's useful about this?
- What can we learn about this?
- How can we make sure we stay on track?[15]

Hewlett-Packard Laboratories recently asked itself, "What would it mean to be the world's best industrial research lab?" The company quickly saw how a big, strategic question galvanized the organization. The director of HP Laboratories began sharing this question with lab employees around the world. She encouraged organization-wide webs of inquiry and conversation, asking people what WBIRL (world's best industrial research lab) meant to them, what it would mean personally for their own jobs, and what it might take to get there. She invited the entire organization to join in exploring the question, first through informal, ongoing conversations and then by way of a more formal internal survey and communications infrastructure. The conversation continued for several months. A creative "reader theater" piece, which reflected eight hundred survey responses detailing employee frustrations, dreams, insights, and hopes, was then developed. Players spoke the key themes as voices of the organization, with senior management listening. Project directors helped the parts to see the whole, and the linking of people with complementary ideas together.

Robert Knowling Jr., who has served as CEO of Internet Access Technologies and Covad Communications, says that he uses questions about the future to shape the organizational vision: "Thinking about what future success looks like is the catalyst for visioning."[16] Some of the questions Knowling uses are:

- How successful will our business be?
- What will the corporate culture be like?
- How will the business be viewed in the industry?

LEADING ORGANIZATIONAL CHANGE

When we use questions to engage the organization's stakeholders and shape our strategic vision and values, it often becomes apparent that the organization needs to change in ways large and small. Pursuing a new vision and a new strategy cannot be accomplished by following the business-as-usual approaches that worked in the past. So, in many organizations, leaders put together a program to sell the needed changes to the organization. This approach usually meets strong resistance.

John P. Kotter, an authority on leading change, says, "According to most assessments, few of these [change] efforts accomplish their goals. Fewer than 15 of the 100 or more companies I have studied have successfully transformed themselves."[17] One problem, he says, is that leaders think change is about "writing a memo," or simply telling the organization to change. "Too often leaders launch their initiatives by calling a meeting or circulating a consultant's report, then expect people to rally to the cause. It doesn't happen that way."

Eric Charoux, executive director of DCDM Business School in Mauritius, found a better way. He realized he faced a choice in dealing with resistance to his plans for the school. "In setting up our governance policies and structures," he told me, "we began to encounter many obstacles, both from a resources and a psychological point of view. In handling these obstacles, we had two options: either the use of a top-down, forceful approach geared to overcoming them and implementing the required change—or the use of questions." He says that he and his colleagues realized that the use of questions would be the wiser choice:

"We began therefore to practice the discipline of asking questions as and when needed. We have found that asking questions generates further explorations, dispels confusion, brings about clarity, transforms conflict into confusion, empowers others, and changes frustration into satisfaction. Above all, questions generate commitment."

The extent to which change is embraced within an organization depends on how adept the leader is at engaging the staff in designing the organization's response to change. Effective leaders use questions to both motivate and guide the change effort. A question calls for an answer, so it acts as a catalyst to fresh thinking and helps to initiate new action.[18] By exploring some of the opportunities posed by strategically asked questions, staff can find new paths to explore for themselves and continue the development of their own careers. Effective leaders pose strategic questions and challenge their people to pursue the answers. Goldberg notes how questions create new openings, whereas statements and opinions rarely do.[19] Statements tend to lead to rote action. Effective questions, on the other hand, lead to effective action; ineffective or neglected questions result in detours, missed goals, and costly mistakes.

Rosabeth Moss Kanter says that change efforts require leaders to use questions to challenge the prevailing organizational wisdom:

> Leaders need to develop what I call kaleidoscope thinking—a way of constructing patterns from the fragments of data available, and then manipulating them to form different patterns. They must question their assumptions about how pieces of the organization, the marketplace, or the community fit together. Change leaders remember that there are many solutions to a problem and that by looking through a different lens somebody is going to invent, for instance, a new way to deliver health care.[20]

When leaders use questions to promote change, they demonstrate that they do not have all the answers and that they are willing to change themselves. This sends a powerful signal. Consider Cindy Stewart's experience:

> When I became the CEO of the Family Health Council of Central Pennsylvania, Inc. in 1999, I needed to shift the culture from a task-oriented hierarchy to a functional, empowered team environment. By leading through questions, I was able to act as a role model and demonstrate my willingness to learn, my desire to serve, and that humility can be inspiring. My employees have come to understand that I am a consultative leader and that it is critical to our success that they are knowledgeable of their customer expectations, willingly

bring key information to the work process, and seek opportunity for continuous quality improvement.

When leading change, *how* questions are often the most powerful. We know where we want to go; the issue is *how to get there*. Frances Hesselbein of the Leader to Leader Institute suggests that leaders focus on *how* questions such as these: "How can we challenge the status quo—doing things *The Way?* How do we meet greater needs with diminishing resources? How do we bridge the divide between the field and the national organization?" She adds, "In these turbulent times, the questions we ask are almost more significant than the responses."[21] *How* questions empower others to find the way.

Gidget Hopf also uses *how* questions to shape a strategic vision at the Association for the Blind and Visually Impaired—Goodwill Industries in Rochester, New York. The questions she used recently included these:

- How can we assure a prominent role for our mission in our quest for financial sustainability?
- How can the board hold staff accountable while not micromanaging?
- How can we more effectively communicate with the board about the difficult environment in which we try to develop new business?

Organizations that create learning environments make change a part of organizational life: after all, learning means changing. And as leaders, we can create agile, change-friendly organizations by asking questions and by encouraging a questioning culture throughout the organization.

QUESTIONS TRANSFORM ORGANIZATIONS

Questions have the power to transform organizations large and small. They can connect us to customers, markets, vendors, the community, and other stakeholders as we shape strategy. *How* questions can shape organizational values and bring commitment to them, and agile companies use questions to promote change.

"As we question and listen," Douglas Eden told me, "we develop credibility with the customers and build solid business relations. If we ask good questions and really listen, the solutions we select really work. We need to be humble, admitting we do not know all the answers, and thus we ask questions."

QUESTIONS FOR REFLECTION

1. How can I change the culture of the organization?
2. What questions can I ask to transform the vision and values of the organization?
3. What questions will enable the organization to adapt to the rapidly changing environment?
4. How do I use questions to bring fresh perspectives in the organization?
5. What questions could I ask to expand the business of the organization?
6. How can I better engage and empower customers and/or clients through questions?
7. How could we use technology to better communicate with our stakeholders?

8. How can I better connect the entire business chain with questions?
9. How can I build greater collaboration with partners through questions?
10. What questions can I use to transform my organization?

Conclusion: Becoming a Questioning Leader

Almost everyone has heard the adage, *You become what you think about*. What is perhaps even more true is that *we become what we ask about*. The people who are most successful in life do not get to the top because of what happens to them or what statements they make to others; they get to the top because of how they question what happens to them and the people and environment around them.

John Kotter, possibly one of the most quoted experts on the subject of leadership, writes that the primary difference between leaders and managers is that leaders are those who ask the right questions whereas managers are those tasked to answer those questions.[1] Asking the right questions enables leaders to discover what is the right thing to do; answering them allows managers to do the right thing.

The importance and power of leading with questions is the theme of this book. Knowing when, where, why, and how to ask questions can help leaders strengthen relationships with staff, build powerful teams, create a strong learning culture, build relationships with customers and other stakeholders, and support strategic change. More than that, when we make asking questions a standard practice, it changes us.

ASKING QUESTIONS CHANGES US

Earlier chapters have emphasized the power of questions on those around the leader. However, questions have an impact on the leader as well. Questions help the questioners find a better understanding of themselves, comprehend more clearly why they do the things they do, and clarify their thinking. To operate in the world from the powerful position of a continuously developing learner, as Adams notes, one must develop a questing mindset.[2] As Alcoa's Michael Coleman says, "My questions obviously impact me as leader. I see [asking questions] as the key way to gain knowledge. It has given me more confidence."

Kouzes and Posner explain how questions help us escape the trap of our own paradigms by broadening our perspectives and helping us to take responsibility for our own viewpoints.[3] Zuboff remarks that we are "prisoners of our organizational vocabulary."[4] Words can either trap us into a particular way of thinking about our roles and relationships or free us for wonderful new opportunities.

Questioning leaders are able to let go of their ego-driven need to have their own answers. They drop their need to be right, so they can allow others to be right. They drop their protective barriers and are more open and vulnerable. Leaders who lead with questions are more easily able to drop their masks and facades and just be who they really are. Questions and answers work for those who are confident and flexible enough to make them work.

Naguib Mahfouz, an Egyptian writer who won the Nobel Prize in Literature, wrote, "You can tell whether a man is clever by his answers. However, you can tell whether a man is *wise* by his questions." Edgar Schein, in his latest book, *Helping*, writes that the "most important challenge for leaders of the 21st century is to learn humble inquiry, by which I mean that leaders of the future will be more and more dependent on their subordinates and will have to learn how to ask for help and to create a climate where subordinates will tell the truth and be helpful."[5]

Questions help us redirect our mindset toward helping the other person achieve. This goes beyond the traditional notion of looking for growth opportunities in other people. Leaders who lead with questions recognize that they do not have all the answers. The resulting humility can be very powerful in being of service to others. Questions help us see that we can lead more effectively by serving than by directing. When you ask questions, you show that you are committed to giving others the opportunity to lead you.

Paul Sloane, author of *The Innovative Leader*, suggests that at the end of the day leaders should ask themselves these five short questions:

1. What was the best thing that happened to me today?
2. What could I have done better today?

3. What is the most important thing I must accomplish tomorrow?

4. What new thing can I try tomorrow?

5. Who is the most important person (or most important people) in my life and what am I doing for them?[6]

BECOMING A LEADER WHO ASKS QUESTIONS

When you move abruptly from being a leader who makes statements to one who asks questions, it may appear disconcerting, at least initially, to your colleagues—particularly your subordinates. How then can you practice inquiry leadership and become more comfortable with and better at asking questions? Marilee Adams suggests the following steps:

1. Start by becoming more aware of the questions you ask now and of the questions other people ask of you. Notice what works. We tend to answer reflexively, not thoughtfully—but effective questioning happens with conscious effort.

2. Try this simple experiment. Pick an hour and force yourself to *not* ask questions. This will focus your attention on the importance of questions. We tend to find ourselves asking questions mentally even if we are not voicing them.

3. Ask yourself more questions silently. Think about your thinking. As you become a conscious observer of your own thinking, you can shape it more intentionally, which will lead you to construct better, more effective questions that will lead to better answers and actions. For example, consciously ask yourself questions such as: What does this mean? Do I

agree or disagree? How could this be helpful? How does this situation fit, contradict, or extend what I already believe to be true?

4. Before asking someone else a question, ask yourself this question: What do I want my question to accomplish? Intentionally frame your question so that you encourage collaborative thinking and cannot be perceived as threatening.

5. Encourage staff to ask you questions. This will, of course, lead to better thinking and actions.

LEADING WITH QUESTIONS IN THE TWENTY-FIRST CENTURY

John F. Kennedy, at his inaugural address in 1961, called on Americans to ask a different kind of question when he spoke these words: "Ask not what your country can do for you—ask what you can do for your country." Questions have an amazing degree of power, and Kennedy's exhortation to Americans on that cold January morning in Washington, D.C.—to ask what they could do for their country—inspired an entire generation to reconsider their values and priorities, to serve others more than to be served. Questions can indeed be that powerful. They are surely the most powerful tool that leaders can possibly employ, for they can accomplish enormous results: questions have the potency and force to change individuals, groups, organizations, communities, even nations and the world.

The effective leaders of the future will need to consistently ask questions to receive feedback and to solicit new ideas. They will ask a variety of stakeholders for ideas, opinions,

243

and feedback. Questions will be seen as a vital source of information for potential customers, suppliers, team members, cross-divisional people, direct reports, managers, other members of the organization, researchers, and thought leaders. The leaders will ask in a variety of ways: through leadership inventories, satisfaction surveys, phone calls, voice mail, e-mail, the Internet, satellite hookups, and in-person dialogue.

Leaders of the future will be more comfortable asking questions of their followers. They will encourage thought and guide with questions rather than answers. They will be open and honest, avoiding the appearance of being know-it-alls. Leaders of the future will be far more skilled at the art of questions than at the art of answering. Practicing this art demands levels of honesty and empowerment that are unknown in many of today's leaders. It is through this art that leaders can begin to share the burden of leadership with their followers, thereby increasing the capacity and performance of the organization.

Leaders who can ask, process information, and learn in a highly efficient manner will build organizations that have a tremendous competitive advantage over their slower and less proactive competition. Leaders who lead with questions will create a more humane workplace as well as a more successful business. Leaders who use questions can truly empower people and change organizations. My hope is that the readers of this book will transform their style of leading from one of statements to one of questions, and thereby become successful and fulfilled as leaders in the twenty-first century.

QUESTIONS FOR REFLECTION

Great leaders ask great questions, and great questions can help me become a great leader.

1. How can I ask great questions?
2. How can I become a great leader by asking great questions?

Resource A:
Biographies of Leaders Interviewed

Shamir Ally is president and CEO of International Consulting and Financial Services. A native of Guyana, he has nearly thirty years of experience in a variety of industries, including electronics, apparel, printing and packaging, insurance, pharmaceuticals, and minerals.

Frank Andracchi recently retired as vice president of Constellation Generation Group. He had been in the power industry since 1969, as an engineer, construction supervisor, division manager, plant manager, and regional manager. Prior to joining Constellation, Frank was a regional manager for resource recovery operations for Ogden Allied Services and spent nineteen years with Long Island Lighting Company.

Jeff Carew has worked at Collectcorp since January 1992, starting as a junior collector at $1,200 per month. He is now vice president of collections. Collectcorp serves major credit grantors in the United States and Canada and has more than 650 employees.

Eric Charoux is a partner at De Chazal Du Mée and executive director of DCDM Business School in Mauritius. Eric has extensive experience assessing and developing executives, managers, and supervisors in Africa, having worked with large organizations in Botswana, South Africa, Swaziland, and Zimbabwe.

Peter Cheng, cofounder of PACE OD Consulting in Singapore, has trained thousands of leaders throughout Asia and Europe. Peter has recently developed the Leading with Questions Academy.

Mike Coleman, vice president of the Alcoa Rigid Packaging business unit in Knoxville, Tennessee, is responsible for Alcoa's aluminum can recycling activities. He is a member of Alcoa's Executive Council, the senior leadership group that provides strategic direction for the company. Prior to joining Alcoa in 1998, Mike was president of North Star Steel. He serves on the board of directors of the Steel Manufacturers' Association and on the executive committee of the Association of Iron and Steel Engineers.

Doug Eden began his career with Cargill in 1978 as a staff accountant in Minneapolis. He served in senior management positions in Thailand and Australia as well as eight cities in the United States before becoming president of Malt Americas.

Ron Edmondson is pastor of Immanuel Baptist Church in Lexington, Kentucky, and has over thirty years of leadership experience as a business owner and as a pastor. He is the founder of Mustard Seed Ministry.

Jean-Paul Gaillard is president of the Ethical Coffee Company. He previously served as CEO of Movenpick Foods and Nestlé USA as well as marketing manager of Philip Morris Europe and Warner Electric.

Mark Harper is currently president of wholesale marketing for ConocoPhillips Petroleum in the United States. He has more than twenty-four years of marketing experience, ranging from packaged goods to food service to petroleum marketing. His prior employers include British Petroleum, Tosco, and Phillips Petroleum.

Robert Hoffman is executive director for organization development at Novartis, where he has worked since 2001. Prior to joining Novartis, Bob spent twelve years with Warner-Lambert, serving in a variety of corporate human resources positions.

Chad Holliday is chairman of the board and CEO of DuPont. Chad is the eighteenth executive to lead the company in the more than two hundred years of DuPont history. Chad is past chairman of the World Business Council for Sustainable

Development (WBCSD) and has coauthored *Walking the Talk*, a book that details the business case for sustainable development and corporate responsibility.

Gidget Hopf, president and CEO of the Association for the Blind and Visually Impaired—Goodwill Industries in Rochester, New York, has spent her entire career in the field of disabilities, first with people who are developmentally disabled and since 1986 with people who are blind. The Rochester program provides comprehensive rehabilitation, career, and training services. It has a food services business as well as a manufacturing division employing eighty people who are blind or visually impaired. Gidget has a doctoral degree in human resource development from George Washington University.

Pam Iorio is a political leader who served as mayor of Tampa, Florida, from 2003 to 2011. She is the author of *Straightforward: Ways to Live and Lead* and a motivational keynote speaker on the subject of leadership.

Tom Laughlin is president of Caravela Inc., an international leadership and team development consulting firm based in Minneapolis, Minnesota. He has served as marketing director in the Baking Products Division at General Mills and has also held management positions in sales, production, and general operations in a number of start-up companies.

Rick Lendemann is the associate dean of Facilities College, Sodexho University, where he manages an action learning accredited degree program. He is a graduate of Brigham

Young University in Provo, Utah, with a bachelor of science degree in Latin American studies.

Suzanne Milchling is head of the Homeland Defense Business Unit, Department of Defense, whose mission is to enhance the response capabilities of military, federal, state, and local emergency responders to terrorist incidents involving weapons of mass destruction.

Kook-Hyun Moon, president and CEO of Yuhan-Kimberly, is well known for his leading by questions. During his twenty-nine years at the company, Moon has used various methods of questioning. Yuhan-Kimberly is known as one of the most admired companies in Korea and won the Best Employer in Asia Award in 2003.

Charles Ostland recently retired after twenty-five years' experience as a teacher before becoming principal of Oakton (Virginia) High School in 1999 where he managed a staff of 220, including nearly 160 teachers.

Jeanette Partlow is president of Maryland Chemical Company, Inc. Customer markets include food and beverage; environmental protection and remediation; metal working; chemical, pharmaceuticals, and electronics manufacturing; and other general industrial applications. She is currently leading a culture transition to a performance management system and a new generation of owner-managers.

Effendy Mohamed Rajab is the senior training and development director for the World Organization of the Scout

Movement, headquartered in Geneva, Switzerland. There are currently 154 National Scout Organizations in the world. Effendy worked as a senior fire and security officer in a petrochemical complex for nineteen years before becoming executive director of the Singapore Scouts Association in 2000.

Isabel Rimanoczy is a partner with LIM (Leadership in International Management) and has authored numerous articles based on her work in Latin America, Europe, the United States, and Asia. She trained more than 150 learning coaches and coauthored the *Learning Coach Handbook*, the *Leader Coach Handbook*, and the *Mergers and Acquisitions Integration Handbook*.

David Rock is cofounder of the NeuroLeadership Institute and CEO of NeuroLeadership Group, a global consulting and training firm with operations in twenty-four countries. He is the author of numerous books, including *Coaching with the Brain in Mind* and *Quiet Leadership*.

David Smyk has more than twenty years' experience in corporate treasury, financial reporting, accounts receivable collections, credit extension, and human resource management with firms such as Aetna Healthcare, Philips, Polaroid, and Sharp Electronics. In 2001, he became a partner in a sales and strategic thinking firm called Healthcare Executive Partners.

Cindy Stewart is president and CEO of the Family Health Council of Central Pennsylvania. Previously she was president and CEO of Family Service of Lancaster County and executive director of the Welsh Mountain Medical and Dental Center, a community health center located in rural Lancaster County. Cindy currently serves as chairman of the Lancaster County Housing & Redevelopment Authority and as president of the Pennsylvania Society of Association Executives.

J. Mike Stice is CEO of Access Midstream Partners, an Oklahoma-based oil and gas company. Mike previously spent twenty-seven years with ConocoPhillips, including serving as president of ConocoPhillips Qatar.

Pentti Sydänmaanlakka has a wide range of experience in all areas of human resource management in Europe, the United States, and Asia. From 1993, he worked as a director of human resources in Nokia Networks. In 2002 he started his own consultancy, Pertec Consulting. He has also been chairman of the Finnish Association of Human Resource Management and has worked for Nixdorf Computer, Siemens Nixdorf Information Systems, Kone Corporation, and VIA Group. He is the author of *An Intelligent Organization*.

Mark Thornhill became CEO of the Midwest Region of the American Red Cross in January 2002. Prior to this, Mark served as chief administrative officer and director of donor services of the New York–Penn Region, where he led that region in its successful 28 percent increase in whole blood collections, and a nearly 300 percent increase in AB plasma collection. Prior to leading the New York–Penn Region, Mark served as director of donor resources and director of manufacturing and distribution in the Alabama Region in Birmingham.

Jayan Warrier is codirector of the World Institute for Action Learning-Singapore as well as the director of Latitude Leadership. He works with organizations in areas of talent and leadership development.

Sue Whitt has more than twenty-five years of corporate leadership experience and consulting expertise. She has held a wide variety of senior leadership roles in the pharmaceutical industry, including positions at Warner-Lambert Parke-Davis, Pfizer, and Abbott Labs.

Resource B:
Action Learning

A Powerful Training Program for Developing Questioning Leaders

When in an epoch of change, when tomorrow is necessarily different from yesterday, new ways of thinking must emerge. New questions need to be asked before solutions are sought. [Leaders need] . . . to learn how to ask appropriate questions under conditions of risk rather than find answers to questions that have already been defined by others. We have to act ourselves into a new way of thinking rather than think ourselves into a new way of acting.

—*Reg Revans, father of action learning*

Now that you have learned how asking the right questions underpins your own success as a leader, you may be wondering how to foster a deeply ingrained culture of questioning across the leadership in your organization. To achieve this, one of the most valuable tools available to you and your team is action learning. Action learning requires individuals and group members to find solutions to problems by asking questions in conditions of risk. By developing the question-based skills of action learning, anyone can become adept at identifying and asking the questions that will make them better leaders.

HOW ACTION LEARNING DEVELOPS QUESTIONING LEADERS

Action learning is built around a group that learns while it solves a problem. At every action learning session, each group member identifies practices and receives feedback on the member's chosen leadership skill. Because the asking of questions is a fundamental in action learning, all the members are continuously demonstrating and improving their questioning competencies.

In recognition of action learning's innate ability to develop inquiring leaders, more and more organizations around the world are using action learning as the primary method for developing leaders. Novartis, Nokia, Samsung, Wells Fargo, Siemens, Boeing, Sony Music, Microsoft, and Panasonic are among the many companies that have made action learning the centerpiece of their leadership development programs. Academic institutions such as American University, Business School of the Netherlands, Harvard University, University of Pretoria, and Salford University have made action learning the cornerstone of their executive leadership programs.

WHAT ARE THE ESSENTIAL ELEMENTS OF ACTION LEARNING?

Briefly defined, action learning is a process that involves people in a small group working on real problems and taking action, so that they learn as individuals, as a team, and as an organization while doing so.[1] Action learning has six components:

1. *A problem*. Action learning centers around a problem—a project, challenge, issue, or task—the resolution of which is of high importance to an individual, team, and/or organization. The problem should be significant and urgent and should be the responsibility of the team to solve. It should also provide an opportunity for the group to ask great questions, to generate learning opportunities, to build knowledge, and to develop individual, team, and organizational skills.

2. *An action learning group*. The core entity in action learning is the action learning group (also called a *set* or *team*). The group is ideally composed of four to eight individuals who examine an organizational problem that has no easily identifiable solution. The group should have diversity of background and experience so as to include various perspectives and to encourage fresh viewpoints and questions.

3. *A process that emphasizes insightful questioning and reflective listening*. Action learning emphasizes questions and reflection over statements and opinions. By focusing on the right questions rather than the right answers, action learning brings out what one does not know as well as what one does know. Participants ask questions to clarify the exact nature of the problem and reflect and identify possible solutions; only then do they take action. The focus is on questions because great solutions are contained within the seeds of great questions. Questions are used to build group dialogue and cohesiveness, generate innovative and systems thinking, and enhance learning results.

4. *A requirement for action*. Action learning requires that the group be able to take action on the problem it is working on. Members of the action learning group must have the

power to take action themselves or be assured that their recommendations will be implemented, barring any significant change in the environment or the group's obvious lack of essential information. Action enhances learning because it provides a basis and anchor for the critical dimension of reflection. The *action* of action learning begins with taking steps to reframe the problem and determine the goal, and only thereafter determining strategies and taking action.

5. *A commitment to learning.* Solving an organizational problem provides immediate short-term benefits to the company. The greater longer-term multiplier benefit, however, is the learning gained by each group member as well as by the group as a whole, and how those insights are applied on a system-wide basis throughout the organization. Thus the learning that occurs in action learning has greater value strategically for the organization than the immediate tactical advantage of early problem correction. Accordingly, action learning places as much emphasis on the learning and development of leaders and the team as it does on the solving of problems; the smarter the group becomes, the quicker and better will be the quality of its decision making and the action it takes.

6. *An action learning coach.* Coaching is necessary for the group to focus on the important (that is, the learning) as well as the urgent (resolving the problem). The action learning coach helps the team members reflect on both what they are learning and how they are solving problems. Through a series of questions, the coach enables group members to reflect on how

258

they listen, how they may have reframed the problem, how they give each other feedback, how they are planning and working, and what assumptions may be shaping their beliefs and actions. The learning coach also helps the team focus on what they are achieving, what they are finding difficult, and what processes they are employing and the implications of these processes. The coaching role may be rotated among members of the group or assigned to one person who holds that role throughout the duration of the group's existence.

HOW DOES AN ACTION LEARNING PROGRAM WORK?

Action learning groups may meet once or several times, depending on the complexity of the problem and the time available for its resolution. The action learning session may take place for one entire day, for a few hours over a few days, or over several months. A group may handle one or many problems. Whatever the time frame, however, action learning generally operates along the following stages and procedures:

1. *Formation of the group*: The group may be volunteer or appointed, and it may be working on a single organizational problem or each other's departmental problems. The group may have a predetermined amount of time and sessions or it may determine the time parameters at the first meeting.

2. *Presentation of problem or task to the group*: The problem is briefly presented to the group by the problem presenter, who

may remain as a member of the group or withdraw and await the group's recommendations.

3. *Reframing the problem*: After a series of questions, the group, often with the guidance of the action learning coach, will reach a consensus as to the most critical and important problem that the group should work on and establish the crux of the problem, which may differ from the original presenting problem.

4. *Determining goals*: Once the key problem or issue has been identified, the group, again through the use of questions, seeks consensus for the goal whose achievement would solve the reframed problem for the long term with positive rather than negative consequences for the individual, team, or organization.

5. *Developing action strategies*: Much of the time and energy of the group will be spent on identifying and pilot-testing possible action strategies. Like the preceding stages of action learning, strategies are developed via questions and reflective dialogue.

6. *Taking action*: Between action learning sessions, the group as a whole as well as individual members collect information, identify the status of support, and implement the strategies developed and agreed to by the group.

7. *Capturing learnings*: Throughout and at any point during the sessions, the action learning coach may intervene to ask the group members questions that will enable them to find ways to improve their performance as a group, to develop their leadership skills, and to identify how their learnings can be applied to their organization and to their lives.

HOW AND WHY ACTION LEARNING DEVELOPS INQUIRY LEADERSHIP

Dilworth notes that leadership development programs, as practiced by most organizations, "produce individuals who are technologically literate and able to deal with intricate problem-solving models, but are essentially distanced from the human dimensions that must be taken into account. Leaders thus may become good at downsizing and corporate restructuring, but cannot deal with a demoralized workforce and the resulting longer-term challenges."[2] Action learning differs from normal leadership development programs in that it requires the individuals and group members to ask appropriate questions in conditions of risk, rather than to find answers that have already been precisely defined by others.[3]

Most management development programs focus on a single dimension. By contrast, action learning derives its power from the fact that it does not isolate any dimension from the context in which the managers work. Instead, it develops the whole leader for the whole organization. What leaders learn and how they learn cannot be dissociated from one another, for *how* one learns necessarily influences *what* one learns. The *how* of action learning is through the mode of questioning.

Learning cannot be solely the acquisition of existing knowledge. Managers need also to improve their ability to search the unfamiliar. Dilworth notes that action learning provides leadership skills that encourage fresh thinking, and thus it enables leaders to avoid responding to today's problems with

261

yesterday's solutions while tomorrow's challenges engulf them. Action learning enables managers to take "appropriate levels of responsibility in discovering how to develop themselves."[4]

Mumford believes action learning is so effective in developing leaders because it incorporates three crucial elements in management development:

1. Taking action leads to more learning than can be derived from merely diagnosing and analyzing or recommending action, as most leadership development programs do.
2. Working on projects that are significant and meaningful to the managers themselves creates greater learning for them than they'd get from going through the motions on abstract problems.
3. Leaders learn better from one another than from instructors who are not managers or who have never managed.[5]

A key outcome of action learning is the development of leaders who incorporate questioning as an integral way of leading. In action learning, everyone receives ample time to practice and demonstrate the art of asking questions. Questions are at the heart of action learning and contribute immensely to its success. With the guidance of the action learning coach, the group reflects on the quality and impact of each individual's questions as well as those of the group. In action learning, finding the right question is more important than answering the wrong question (no matter how well it is answered). This habit of questioning others as well as oneself represents a unique strength of action learning.[6]

The primary way in which action learning differs from other leadership programs and problem-solving approaches is its focus on questions rather than on solutions. Only through questions can a group truly gain a common understanding of the problem, acquire a sense of each member's potential strategies, and achieve innovative breakthrough strategies and solutions. Questions, when asked at the right time in the right way, provide the glue that brings and holds the group together. To use another metaphor, the seeds of the answer are contained in the questions. Thus the better the questions, the better the solutions—and the learning; the deeper the reflection, the greater the development of individual and team competencies.

Questions serve many purposes for action learning groups. They enable members to understand, to clarify, and to open up new avenues of exploration for solving the problem. They provide new insights and ideas for strategic actions and potential paths for solutions. Questions build understanding while laying the groundwork for gaining support for possible action. Questions also serve as the foundation for individual, team, and organizational learning, and especially for the development of inquiring leaders.

QUESTIONS FIRST IN ACTION LEARNING

Much of the potency of action learning comes from questions that generate reflective inquiry. Therefore action learning groups and the action learning coach are strongly encouraged to establish this ground rule during their sessions: *statements can be made only in response to a question.*

This ground rule does not prohibit the use of statements; as a matter of fact, there may still be more statements than questions during the action learning meetings, because every question asked may generate one or more responses from each of the other members of the group, or as many as five to ten statements per question.

However, by requiring people to think "questions first," the entire dynamics of the group is transformed. The natural impulse to make statements and judgments changes to one of listening and reflecting. Once the problem or task has been introduced to the group, the members must first ask questions to clarify the problem before jumping into statements solving the problem. In action learning, we recognize that there is an almost direct correlation between the number and quality of questions and the eventual quality of the final actions and learnings. Balancing the number of questions and the number of statements leads to dialogue, which is a proper balance between advocating and inquiring.

This ground rule provides tremendous value to the action learning group. First, it forces everyone in the group to think about asking questions, about inquiring rather than making statements and advocating positions. Questions tend to unite; statements can cause divisions. An environment in which questions are valued requires people to listen to each other. Questions prevent domination by a single person and instead create cohesion.

Two questions are often raised about this ground rule. First, doesn't this ground rule limit the free flow of interaction among group members? Yes, it may slow down the rapid flow of communication, but in action learning this is seen as a positive as it forces members to be more reflective and creative, to listen first. Second, won't some people be able to manipulate this rule, and merely raise the pitch of their voice at the end of a statement and thereby convert it into a question? This is certainly possible, but once any statement is converted into a question, the power then moves to the respondents, who may choose to agree or not agree, may choose to reflect upon the question, or may respond with a more open question of their own.

Action learning members quickly become comfortable and competent in this approach to communications. As action learning groups experience the tremendous benefits of questioning, they gladly embrace this precept. It recaptures their natural way of communicating and learning—the one they used as toddlers, before it got stamped out by the adults who kept saying, "Stop asking so many questions!" The quality of the group's work and the comfort of the interactions often inspire members to apply this ground rule in other parts of organizational life.

In most problem-solving situations, only the knowledge that is brought into the group by its members is considered and applied. This limited knowledge allows for only an incremental, narrowly focused understanding and limited solutions to the problem; it rarely generates the quantum improvements or spectacular leaps in knowledge necessary to solve today's more complex problems. Programmed knowledge alone is simply inadequate to solving problems from a systems perspective.

Only through questions and reflections (that is, the reflective inquiry process of action learning) can a group generate a holistic, broad-based perspective. By seeing each other as learners and learning resources, members of an action learning group anticipate the generation of new knowledge within the group. Questioning builds on the knowledge that people bring into the group while at the same time constructing new knowledge and learning.

By beginning with questioning rather than using past knowledge as the first reference point, the group can gauge whether the information presently available is adequate and relevant to the situation. The key to problem solving is to start with fresh questions, not constructs and assumptions from the past. Questions enable groups to unpeel the layers around the problem and uncover the core elements of knowledge necessary to discover the solution.

THE ACTION LEARNING COACH AS A QUESTIONING LEADER

The skills and practice of leading with questions can be developed in action learning in the group member role, but they develop even more powerfully when the leader takes a turn as coach. A number of important questioning skills, values, and attributes are developed in serving as an action learning coach:

• *Ability to ask questions.* The key skill of the action learning coach is the ability to ask good questions, both initial and especially follow-up questions. The coach needs to be able to ask questions that make people think and feel challenged; the questions should be supportive and positive rather than critical. To consistently ask good questions, the action learning coach needs a strong and sincere belief in the power of questions and the critical role of the action learning coach in asking questions. The manner of introducing questions should be gentle and not arrogant, so the coach needs to look inward and determine whether a chosen question will be truly helpful to the group, one that could create possibilities for significant learning and breakthrough action.

• *Courage and authenticity.* Asking questions is not always easy, especially the tough follow-up questions or questions that require deep and intensive soul-searching. The action learning coach needs to be courageous and authentic, strong and unintimidated by the rank or expertise or character of the person to whom the question is posed, and willing to pursue doubts about the existence of agreement or clarity.

• *A sense of timing.* Finding the ideal time for intervening is an art for the action learning coach. Intervene too early, and the group or individual may not have enough experience to have developed sufficient data to respond adequately, and thus may miss an opportunity for understanding. Intervene too late, and the group's overlong struggle may lead to frustration and a missed opportunity for learning. Experience will make the coach grow more comfortable and confident in intervention timing. And, though timing is important, any time that one intervenes can be an occasion of great learning.

• *Confidence and trust in the process and the people in the group.* The action learning coach must be confident in the role and must demonstrate this confidence by displaying a relaxed belief in the action learning process and the eventual success of the group. The coach should radiate assurance that the action learning process will work, that the theories and principles underlying it (namely, the six components and two rules) are demonstrably sound. The coach should believe that everyone in the group has abilities necessary to solve the problem, so the coach's job is merely to bring out and capitalize on these strengths: to get the group from today to tomorrow. With a strong confidence in the success of the process and the people, the action learning coach is able to tolerate ambiguity more easily.

• *Values and characteristics.* The action learning coach, because of the power inherent in the role, should be cognizant of the way personal values and actions affect the group and the action learning process. By presence alone, the coach has a significant impact on the group; the members know that the coach may raise questions at any point that will challenge their thinking and actions, decisions made and not made. Therefore, a number of characteristics are fitting for an action learning coach, including openness, patience, honesty and integrity, humility, the ability to be nonjudgmental, and the capacity for reflection. Like the leader in Herman Hesse's *Journey to the East*, the action learning coach is so subtle and natural that the group does not realize how powerful and beneficial the coach's influence is. They do not realize its value unless or until they no longer have the coach to rely on.

• *Strong coordination and planning skills.* As noted earlier in this chapter, the action learning coach has a variety of other roles in addition to serving as a coach to an action learning group. These other roles require strong coordination skills and the ability see the big picture and not become lost in details. Because the coach needs to be able to maintain working and supportive relationships with so many people inside and outside the group and even the organization, the role requires the ability to keep many balls in the air at the same time.

• *Good listening skills.* Successful action learning coaches need to possess strong listening skills. They should be able to hear what is not said as well as what is said. Careful observation and good note taking allow them to be in tune with who is saying what, how, when, and to whom. Active listening requires a great deal of attention. This strong listening enables them to acquire a "helicopter-type" perspective and holistic view. They must be able to stand apart from the problem and focus on the development of the group.

• *Strong commitment to learning.* Action learning coaches must be eager to see people learn. As tempting as it may be to do otherwise during the action learning sessions, they focus on the learning, not on the issue or problem being discussed. They understand and appreciate how adults learn and they see learning as a way of life. And they recognize that learners can learn only for themselves.[7]

• *Attitude toward group members.* Effective action learning coaches respect each person and have concern for the well-being of all members. They want everyone to succeed with the project and to learn from so doing. This ability to empathize and be supportive is very important. They should see members as curious and thoughtful about the problem and about each other. These attitudes generate more trust in the coach as well as more openness among the group members.

• *Self-awareness and self-confidence.* Action learning coaches need to be cognizant of their own strengths and limitations, with enough self-confidence to be authentic and resilient. Their humility allows them to demonstrate that they are still willing and able to learn. They should want to be seen as people who can be trusted, who can handle rivalries, distrust, and anger.

Resource C:
Resources for Training and Information on Questioning Leadership

WORLD INSTITUTE FOR ACTION LEARNING (WIAL)

As noted in Resource B, one of the most effective ways to develop questioning skills for leaders is through action learning. The World Institute for Action Learning (WIAL) and its affiliates have trained thousands of leaders around the world via the action learning methodology. WIAL has also developed one-day and two-day Leading with Questions workshops. For more information about receiving training in action learning and in developing questioning skills for leaders, visit the website of the World Institute for Action Learning: www.wial.org.

INQUIRY INSTITUTE

The Inquiry Institute has a number of training programs designed to promote the expert application of inquiry and reflection skills by leaders and managers. Much of the content of these programs is based on a methodology called Question Thinking™ (QT), outlined in Dr. Marilee Adams's international bestselling book *Change Your Questions, Change Your Life: 10 Powerful Tools for Life and Work*. The book focuses on the impact of a leader's mindset and the kinds of questions generated by either a "learner mindset" or a "judger mindset." For information about the Inquiry Institute, visit www.InquiryInstitute.com.

LEADING WITH QUESTIONS ACADEMY/PACE-OD SINGAPORE

The Leading with Questions Academy/PACE-OD offers two-day workshops based on the *Leading with Questions* book. The workshop uses a fusion of experiential activities, business cases, video learning, and interactive activities. For information about the workshop, visit www.pace-od.com.

LEADING WITH QUESTIONS WEBSITE/BLOG

One of the most informative and enjoyable blogs on questioning is authored by Bob Tiede and is free to all subscribers (www.leadingwithquestions.com). Twice a week Bob posts sage advice on his blog to sharpen your "Leading with Questions" skills—drawing on his personal experience as a forty-two-year veteran of Cru (formerly known as *Campus Crusade for Christ*). One of the core skills that he seeks to develop in Cru's emerging leaders is their ability to "Lead with Questions."

Bob's blog is filled with stories of leaders using questions to solve real-life problems. His advice is practical and applicable to your job as a leader. Even if you have been a leader for a long time, you will find yourself challenged to try using questions in ways you haven't thought of before. Many of the top authors on leadership and questions serve as guest bloggers and offer their best questions as well as best advice on leading with questions. Here is just a sampling of recent www.leadingwithquestions.com posts:

- "There is only one question that I ask!"
- Would You Like to Know the Four Questions One Consultant Uses to Make a Six Figure Income?
- Can You Fire Someone by Just Asking Questions?
- How Can We Do This in a Way That Will "Guarantee Its Failure"?
- How to Consult Like Peter Drucker
- Would You Like to Know the 4 Questions That One Specialist Uses to Turn Around Companies/Organizations That Are in Trouble?
- Would You Like to Know How the Walt Disney World Textile Services Lowered Their Annual Employee Turnover Rate from 85% to Less Than 10%?
- My Top Ten Favorite "Leading with Questions" Quotes
- Can You Answer Three Questions Asked by Leo Tolstoy?
- Stop Fixing, Start Coaching

Notes

Introduction

1. Daudelin, M. (1996). "Learning from Experience." *Organization Dynamics, 24*(3), 36–48.

Chapter One

1. Cohen, G. (2009). *Just Ask Leadership: Why Great Managers Always Ask the Right Questions*. New York: McGraw-Hill.
2. Mittelstaedt, R. E. (2005). *Will Your Next Mistake Be Fatal?* Upper Saddle River, NJ: Wharton School, 101.
3. Janis, I. L. (1971). "Groupthink." *Psychology Today, 5*(6), 43–44, 46, 74–76.
4. Ibid., 76.
5. Collins, J. (2001). *Good to Great*. New York: HarperBusiness, 88.
6. Finkelstein, S. (2003). *Why Smart Executives Fail*. New York: Portfolio, 200.
7. Finkelstein, S. (2004, Winter). "Zombie Businesses: How to Learn from Their Mistakes." *Leader to Leader* (32), 25–31.
8. Tichy, N. M., with Cardwell, N. (2002). *The Cycle of Leadership: How Great Leaders Teach Their Companies to Win*. New York: HarperBusiness, 64.
9. Ibid., 60.
10. Ibid.
11. Parker, M. (2001, December). "Breakthrough Leadership." *Harvard Business Review*, 37.
12. Oakley, D., & Krug, D. (1991). *Enlightened Leadership*. New York: Simon & Schuster.
13. Kotter, J. P. (1998, Fall). "Winning at Change." *Leader to Leader* (10), 27–33.
14. Drucker, P., & Maciariello, J. (2004). *The Daily Drucker*. New York: Harper-Business.

15. Mill, J. S. (1998). *On Liberty and Other Essays*. Oxford: Oxford University Press. (Originally published 1859.)
16. Collins, *Good to Great*, 75.
17. Crowley, J. (2004). "Enlightened Leadership in the U.S. Navy." Retrieved from http://enlightenedleadershipsolutions.com/lmd/lmd_articles.html
18. Abrashoff, D. M. (2002). *It's Your Ship: Management Techniques from the Best Damn Ship in the Navy*. New York: Warner Books.
19. Ibid., 33.
20. Tichy, *The Cycle of Leadership*, 61.
21. Ibid.
22. Goldsmith, M. (1996). "Ask, Learn, Follow Up, and Grow." In F. Hesselbein, M. Goldsmith, & R. Beckhard (Eds.), *The Leader of the Future: New Visions, Strategies, and Practices for the Next Era* (pp. 227–237). San Francisco: Jossey-Bass.
23. Ibid., 231.

Chapter Two

1. Goldberg, M. (1998). *The Art of the Question: A Guide to Short-Term Question-Centered Therapy*. New York: Wiley.
2. Tichy, *The Cycle of Leadership*, 61.
3. Block, P. (2003, May). "Strategies of Consent." Handout at 2003 ASTD Conference, Atlanta.
4. Welch, J. (2005). *Winning*. New York: HarperBusiness.
5. Kouzes, J., & Posner, B. (2012). *The Leadership Challenge* (5th ed.). San Francisco: Jossey-Bass, 83.
6. Adams, M. (2004). *Change Your Questions, Change Your Life: 7 Powerful Tools for Life and Work*. San Francisco: Berrett-Koehler.
7. Goldberg, *The Art of the Question*, 8–9.
8. Adams, *Change Your Questions*.
9. Coffman, V. (2002, August). Interview with Lockheed Martin Chairman and CEO Vance Coffman. *Academy of Management Executive, 16*(3), 31–40.
10. Mitroff, I. (1998). *Smart Thinking for Crazy Times: The Art of Solving the Right Problems*. San Francisco: Berrett-Koehler.
11. Block, P. (2012). *The Answer to How Is Yes*. San Francisco: Berrett-Koehler.
12. Vaill, P. (1996). *Learning as a Way of Being: Strategies for Survival in a World of Permanent White Water*. San Francisco: Jossey-Bass.
13. Wheatley, M. (2009). *Turning to One Another: Simple Conversations to Restore Hope to the Future*. San Francisco: Berrett-Koehler.
14. Blanchard, K. (2003). *The Servant Leader*. Nashville, TN: Countryman.
15. Wheatley, *Turning to One Another*.
16. Goldberg, *The Art of the Question*.
17. Vaill, *Learning as a Way of Being*.
18. Goldberg, *The Art of the Question*.
19. Hii, A. (2000). *The Impact of Action Learning on the Conflict-Handling Styles of Managers in a Malaysian Firm*. Unpublished doctoral dissertation, George Washington University.
20. Badaracco, J. (2002). *Leading Quietly*. Boston: Harvard Business School Press.
21. Ibid., 172.

22. Dilworth, L. (1998). "Action Learning in a Nutshell." *Performance Improvement Quarterly*, *11*(1), 28–43.
23. Morris, J. (1991). "Minding Our Ps and Qs." In M. Pedler (Ed.), *Action Learning in Practice*. Aldershot, England: Gower.
24. Collins, *Good to Great* (see chap. 1, n. 5).
25. Badaracco, *Leading Quietly*.
26. Caplan, J. (2006, Oct. 2). "Google's Chief Looks Ahead." *Time*. Retrieved from http://www.time.com/time/business/article/0,8599,1541446,00.html

Chapter Three

1. Semler, R. (1993). *Maverick*. New York: Warner Books.
2. Goldberg, *The Art of the Question*, 9 (see chap. 2, n. 1).
3. Block, "Strategies of Consent" (see chap. 2, n. 3).
4. Bianco-Mathis, V., Nabors, L., & Roman, C. (2002). *Leading from the Inside Out*. Thousand Oaks, CA: Sage.
5. Revans, R. (1982). *The Origins and Growth of Action Learning*. Bromley, England: Chartwell Brat.
6. Heifetz, R., & Linsky, M. (2002). *Leadership on the Line*. Boston: Harvard Business School Press.
7. Goldberg, *The Art of the Question* (see chap. 2, n. 1).
8. Nadler, G., & Chandon, W. (2004). *Smart Questions: Learn to Ask the Right Questions for Powerful Results*. San Francisco: Jossey-Bass.
9. Yankelovich, D. (1999). *The Magic of Dialogue: Transforming Conflict into Cooperation*. New York: Simon & Schuster.
10. Finkelstein, *Why Smart Executives Fail* (see chap. 1, n. 6).
11. Heifetz & Linsky, *Leadership on the Line*.
12. Morris, "Minding our Ps and Qs" (see chap. 2, n. 23).

Chapter Four

1. Kouzes & Posner, *The Leadership Challenge* (see chap. 2, n. 5).
2. Goldberg, *The Art of the Question*, 9 (see chap. 2, n. 1).
3. Revans, *The Origins and Growth of Action Learning* (see chap. 3, n. 5).
4. All Einstein quotes are from www.alberteinsteinsite/com/quotes
5. Senge, P., Roberts, C., Roth, G., Ross, R., & Smith, B. (1999). *The Dance of Change: The Challenges to Sustaining Momentum in Learning Organizations*. New York: Doubleday/Currency.

Chapter Five

1. Adams, *Change Your Questions* (see chap. 2, n. 6). *All subsequent chapter references to Adams refer to this book.*
2. Cooperrider, D., & Whitney, D. (2012). *Appreciative Inquiry*. Champaign, IL: Stipes Press.
3. Whitney, D., Cooperrider, D., Trosten-Bloom, A., & Kaplin, B. (2002). *Encyclopedia of Positive Questions*. Euclid, OH: Lakeshore Communications.
4. Kouzes & Posner, *The Leadership Challenge* (see chap. 2, n. 5).

5. Dillon, J. (1988). *Questioning and Teaching*. New York: Teachers College Press.
6. Leeds, D. (2000). *The Seven Powers of Questions*. New York: Perigee Books.
7. Hesselbein, F. (2005, Winter). "The Leaders We Need." *Leader to Leader* (35), 4–5.
8. Goldsmith, M. (1996). "Ask, Learn, Follow Up, and Grow." In F. Hesselbein, M. Goldsmith, & R. Beckhard (Eds.), *The Leader of the Future: New Visions, Strategies, and Practices for the Next Era* (pp. 227–237). San Francisco: Jossey-Bass.

Chapter Six

1. Clemens, J., & Mayer, D. (1987). *The Classic Touch: Lessons in Leadership from Homer to Hemingway*. Homewood, IL: Irwin.
2. Heimbold, C. (1999). "Attributes and Formation of Good Leaders." *Vital Speeches of the Day, 65*(6), 179–181.
3. Daudelin, "Learning from Experience" (see intro., n. 1).
4. Schein, E. (2004). *Organizational Culture and Leadership* (3rd ed.). San Francisco: Jossey-Bass.
5. Wheatley, *Turning to One Another* (see chap. 2, n. 13).
6. Isaacs, W. (1993, August). "Taking Flight: Dialogue, Collective Thinking and Organizational Learning." *Organizational Dynamics*, 24–39.
7. Wheatley, *Turning to One Another*.
8. Kouzes & Posner, *The Leadership Challenge* (see chap. 2, n. 5).
9. Collins, *Good to Great* (see chap. 1, n. 5).
10. Wheatley, *Turning to One Another*.
11. Clarke-Epstein, C. (2006). *78 Important Questions Every Leader Should Ask and Answer*. New York: AMACOM.
12. Cohen, *Just Ask Leadership* (see chap. 1, n. 1).
13. Schein, *Organizational Culture and Leadership*.

Chapter Seven

1. Sobel, A., & Panas, J. (2012). *Power Questions*. San Francisco: Wiley.
2. Block, "Strategies of Consent" (see chap. 2, n. 3).
3. Whitney, Cooperrider, Trosten-Bloom, & Kaplin, *Encyclopedia of Positive Questions* (see chap. 5, n. 3).
4. Rogers, C. (1961). *On Becoming a Person*. Boston: Houghton Mifflin.
5. Carkhuff, R. (1969). *Helping and Human Relations*. Amherst, MA: HRD Press.
6. Bianco-Mathis, Nabors, & Roman, *Leading from the Inside Out* (see chap. 3, n. 4).
7. Mezirow, J. (1991). *Transformative Dimensions of Adult Learning*. San Francisco: Jossey-Bass.
8. Whitney et al., *Encyclopedia of Positive Questions*.
9. Champy, J. (2000, Summer). "The Residue of Leadership: Why Ambition Matters." *Leader to Leader* (17), 14–19.
10. Schein, *Organizational Culture and Leadership*.
11. Bass, B. (1985). *Leadership and Performance Beyond Expectations*. New York: Free Press.
12. Goldberg, *The Art of the Question* (see chap. 2, n. 1).
13. Vaill, *Learning as a Way of Being* (see chap. 2, n. 12).

14. Hamel, G. (2003). "A New Way of Seeing the World." *Executive Excellence, 20*(2), 16–17.
15. Bossidy, L., & Charan, R. (2002). *Execution: The Discipline of Getting Things Done.* New York: Crown.
16. Hesselbein, F. (2005, Winter). "The Leaders We Need," 5 (see chap. 5, n. 7).
17. Clarke-Epstein, *78 Important Questions Every Leader Should Ask and Answer,* 211 (see chap. 6, n. 11).
18. Goldberg, M. (1998). "The Spirit and Discipline of Organizational Inquiry." *Manchester Review* (3), 1–7.
19. Leeds, *The Seven Powers of Questions* (see chap. 5, n. 6).
20. Clarke-Epstein, *78 Important Questions Every Leader Should Ask and Answer.*
21. Goldsmith, M. (2012). *Coaching for Leadership.* New York: Pfeiffer.
22. Clarke-Epstein, *78 Important Questions.*
23. Vaill, *Learning as a Way of Being* (see chap. 2, n. 12).

Chapter Eight

1. Senge, P. (2006). *The Fifth Discipline.* New York: Doubleday.
2. Peters, T. (1996). *Liberation Management.* New York: Knopf.
3. Wheatley, *Turning to One Another* (see chap. 2, n. 13).
4. Bianco-Mathis et al., *Leading from the Inside Out* (see chap. 3, n. 4).
5. Whitmore, J. (2002). *Coaching for Performance: Growing People, Performance and Purpose.* Yarmouth, ME: Brealey.
6. Lencioni, P. M. (2003, Summer). "The Trouble with Teamwork." *Leader to Leader* (29), 35–40.
7. Mill, J. S. (1998). *On Liberty and Other Essays.* Oxford: Oxford University Press. (Original work published 1859.)
8. Axelrod, R. H., Axelrod, E. M., Beedon, J., & Jacobs, R. W. (2005, Spring). "Creating Dynamic, Energy-Producing Meetings." *Leader to Leader* (36), 53–58.
9. Wheatley, *Turning to One Another.*
10. Axelrod et al., "Creating Dynamic, Energy-Producing Meetings."
11. Levi, D. (2010). *Group Dynamics for Teams.* Thousand Oaks, CA: Sage.
12. Ury, W. (1993). *Getting Past No: Negotiating Your Way from Confrontation to Cooperation.* New York: Bantam Books.

Chapter Nine

1. Merchant, N. (2010). *The New How.* Sebastopol, CA: O'Reilly.
2. Heifetz, R., & Laurie, D. (1997). "The Work of Leadership." *Harvard Business Review, 75*(1), 124–134.
3. Merchant, *The New How.*
4. Cooperrider & Whitney, *Appreciative Inquiry* (see chap. 5, n. 2).
5. Burger, E. B., & Starbird, M. (2012). *The 5 Elements of Effective Thinking.* Princeton, NJ: Princeton University Press.
6. Daudelin, "Learning from Experience" (see intro., n. 1).
7. Bianco-Mathis et al., *Leading from the Inside Out* (see chap. 3, n. 4).

8. Marquardt, M., & Yeo, R. (2012). *Breakthrough Problem Solving with Action Learning*. Palo Alto, CA: Stanford University Press.

Chapter Ten

1. Adams, *Change Your Questions* (see chap. 2, n. 6).
2. Hymowitz, C. (2004, December 28). "Some Tips from CEOs." *Wall Street Journal*, B1.
3. Tiede, B. (2013). Retrieved from http://leadingwithquestions.com
4. Hammer, M. (2001). *What Every Business Must Do to Dominate the Decade*. New York: Crown Business.
5. Drucker, P. F., & Maciariello, J. A. (2004). *The Daily Drucker*. New York: Harper-Business, 367.
6. Clarke-Epstein, *78 Important Questions Every Leader Should Ask and Answer* (see chap. 6, n. 11).
7. Leeds, D. (1987). *Smart Questions: The Essential Strategy for Successful Managers*. New York: McGraw-Hill.
8. Bell, C., & Bell, B. (2003). *Magnetic Service: Secrets of Creating Passionately Devoted Customers*. San Francisco: Berrett-Koehler.
9. Manville, B. (2001, Spring). "Learning in the New Economy." *Leader to Leader* (20), 36–45.
10. Harbison, J. R., & Pekar, P., Jr. (1998, second quarter). "Institutionalizing Alliance Skills: Secrets of Repeatable Success." *strategy+business*. Available online with registration: http://www.strategy-business.com/press/article/15893?pg=0
11. Tischler, L. (2001, December). "Seven Strategies for Successful Alliances." *Fast Company*. Retrieved from http://www.fastcompany.com/64778/seven-strategies-successful-alliances
12. Austin, J. E. (1998, Spring). "The Invisible Side of Leadership." *Leader to Leader* (8), 38–46.
13. Blanchard, K., & Stoner, J. (2011). *Full Steam Ahead*. San Francisco: Berrett-Koehler.
14. Hesselbein, F., Goldsmith, M., & Beckhard, R. (1996). *The Leader of the Future: New Visions, Strategies, and Practices for the Next Era*. San Francisco: Jossey-Bass.
15. Goldberg, *The Art of the Question* (see chap. 2, n. 1).
16. Knowling, R., Jr. (2002). "Leading with Vision, Strategy, and Values." In F. Hesselbein, M. Goldsmith, & I. Somerville (Eds.), *Leading for Innovation*. San Francisco: Jossey-Bass.
17. Kotter, "Winning at Change," 27 (see chap. 1, n. 13).
18. Blohowiak, D. (2000). "Question Your Way to the Top!" *Productive Leader, 121*, 1–3.
19. Goldberg, *The Art of the Question* (see chap. 2, n. 1).
20. Kanter, R. M. (1999, Summer). "The Enduring Skills of Change Leaders." *Leader to Leader* (13), 15–22.
21. Hesselbein, F. (2003, Winter). "Finding the Right Questions." *Leader to Leader* (27), 4–6.

Conclusion

1. Kotter, J. (2002). *The Heart of Change*. Cambridge, MA: Harvard Business School Press.
2. Adams, *Change Your Questions* (see chap. 2, n. 6).
3. Kouzes & Posner, *The Leadership Challenge* (see chap. 2, n. 5).
4. Zuboff, S. (1989). *In the Age of the Smart Machine: The Future of Work and Power*. New York: Basic Books.
5. Schein, E. (2011). *Helping: How to Offer, Give, and Receive Help*. San Francisco: Berrett-Koehler.
6. Sloane, P. (2007). *The Innovative Leader*. London: Kogan Page.

Resource B: Action Learning

1. Marquardt, M. (2004). *Optimizing the Power of Action Learning*. Palo Alto, CA: Davies-Black Publishing.
2. Dilworth, L. (1996). "Action Learning: Bridging Academic and Workplace Domains." *Employee Counseling Today* (6), 48–56.
3. Revans, *The Origins and Growth of Action Learning* (see chap. 3, n. 5).
4. Dilworth, "Action Learning in a Nutshell" (see chap. 2, n. 22).
5. Mumford, A. (1995). "Developing Others Through Action Learning." *Industrial and Commercial Training*, 27(2), 19–27.
6. McNulty, N., & Canty, G. (1995). "Proof of the Pudding." *Journal of Management Education*, 14(1), 53–66.
7. Boud, D., Keogh, R., & Walker, D. (1985). *Reflection: Turning Experience into Learning*. London: Kogan Page.

Acknowledgments

I would like to acknowledge the many people who helped me to ask better questions and thus made my life so rich and wonderful. First, my mother, Elaine, who encouraged me to ask questions and to always strive to learn from those questions. I wish to thank my wife, Eveline, who often asks her husband *why;* and my children, Chris, Stephanie, Catherine, and Emily, who questioned their dad's wisdom, especially during their teenage years. Finally, my nine grandchildren, Kennedy, Ian, Patricia, Hannah, Millie, Maia, Finn, Milo, and Vespa, who have asked me so many wonderful questions with such joy and love.

Over the years, I have been blessed to work with and learn from a number of great leaders; leaders such as Barrie Oxtoby, Kevin Wheeler, Wayne Pace, Charles Margerison, Len Nadler, Kathy Chalmers, Malcolm Knowles, Reg Revans, Nissim Tal, Frank Andracchi, Pierre Gheysons, Arthur Byrnes, Harry Lenderman, Steve King, Tina Sung, Nancy Stebbins, Frank Sofo, Lex Dilworth, and Ila Young. I have learned much about leadership from the questions of my GWU doctoral graduates, many of whom are now successful global leaders—Wong Wee Chwee, Antony Hii, Taebok Lee, Myoung Choi, Mary Tomasello, William Weech, Florence Ho, Effendy Mohammed Rajab, Banu Golesorkhi, Agata Dulnik, Dan Navarro, Doug Bryant, Teo Campos, Stan Surrette, Sung Hae Kim, Marissa Wettasinghe, Robin Hurst, Lorraine Warner, Somsri Siriwaiprapan, Robert Richer, Carla Bowens, Deb Waddill, Bernadette Carson, Millie Mateu, Colleen Richmond, Al McCready, Deb Gmelin, Gidget Hopf, Agata Dulnik, Sooyeon Choi, Taebok Lee, Mohammed Al-Emadi, Brian Williams, Lisa Toppin, Mary Voltz-Peacock, Huda Ayas, Linda Fang, Peng Soon Lim, Charles Tweedly, Mary Ann Wangeman, Ernie Smith, William Toms, Mark Stavish, Pascal Etzol, Al McCready, Casey Lowe, James Lim, Sydney Savion, Milynn Swofford, Kathleen Kueht, Glenn Geelhoed, William Yates, Jeanne Lian, Mitch Wasden, Vareen O'Keefe, Robert Hamilton, Hal Metcalfe, Steve Terrell, Charlotte Barner, Mike Stice, David Estworthy, Rob Bedrosian, Deb Silva, Bobbie Deleon, Simon Reese, Karen Detweiler, Randy Dobson, Tim Hope, Nicole Harris, Dave Rude, Ron Sheffeld, Andrew Rahaman, and Tom Dembeck.

I especially want to thank all the folks at Jossey-Bass/Wiley, particularly Rob Brandt, John Maas, Mark Karmendy, and Genoveva Llosa, who guided the development of this revised and updated book and helped to polish the writing.

And finally, I am truly indebted to the thirty leaders whose questions and wisdom are found throughout this book—wonderful people who patiently answered my questions about their questioning leadership style. These leaders (listed in Resource A) offered so many great questions and ideas; all were an inspiration to me and, I am sure, will be an inspiration for the readers of this book.

About the Author

Michael Marquardt is professor of Human Resource Development and International Affairs as well as program director of the Executive Leadership Program at George Washington University. Mike also serves as president of the World Institute for Action Learning.

He has held a number of senior management, training, and marketing positions with organizations such as Grolier, American Society for Training and Development, Association Management Inc., Overseas Education Fund, TradeTec, and the U.S. Office of Personnel Management. Dr. Marquardt has trained more than 100,000 managers in nearly 150 countries since beginning his international experience in Spain in 1969. Consulting assignments have included Marriott, Microsoft, Sony Music, Goodrich, Motorola, Nortel, Alcoa, Boeing, Caterpillar, United Nations Development Program, Xerox, Nokia, Constellation, Samsung, Organization of American States, and Singapore Airlines as well as the governments of Indonesia, Laos, Ethiopia, Zambia, Egypt, Kuwait, Saudi Arabia, Turkey, Russia, Jamaica, Honduras, and Swaziland.

Dr. Marquardt is the author of twenty-four books and over one hundred professional articles in the fields of leadership, learning, globalization, and organizational change, including *Action Learning for Developing Leaders and Organizations*, *Optimizing the Power of Action Learning*, *Building the Learning Organization* (selected as Book of the Year by the Academy of HRD), *The Global Advantage*, *Action Learning in Action*, *Global Leaders for the 21st Century*, *Global Human Resource Development*, *Technology-Based Learning*, and *Global Teams*. Over one million copies of his publications have been sold in nearly a dozen languages worldwide. Dr. Marquardt also served as the editor of the UNESCO Encyclopedia volume on Human Resources and is an editor and/or advisor for several leading professional journals around the world. He has been a keynote speaker at international conferences in Australia, Japan, the Philippines, Malaysia, South Africa, Singapore, and India as well as throughout North America.

Dr. Marquardt's achievements and leadership have been recognized though numerous awards, including the International Practitioner of the Year Award from the American Society for Training and Development. He presently serves as a senior advisor for the United Nations Staff College in the areas of policy, technology, and learning systems. He is a Fellow of the National Academy for Human Resource Development. His writings and accomplishments in action learning have earned him honorary doctoral degrees from universities in Asia, Europe, and North America.

Dr. Marquardt received his doctorate in human resource development from George Washington University and his master's and bachelor's degrees from Maryknoll College. He has done graduate work at Harvard, Columbia, and the University of Virginia. He enjoys skiing, music, and traveling with his wife, four children, and nine grandchildren.

Index

A

Abrashoff, D. Michael (Commander), 25–27
Acceptance of organizational change, 41–43
Accountability, 187
Action, encouraging, 162–165
Action learning: coaching, 258–259, 266–270; developing inquiry leadership, 261–263; essential elements of, 256–259; groups, 257; how it develops questioning leaders, 256; how it works, 259–260; overview, 255–256; questions first rule, 263–266
Adams, Marilee, 242–243
Adaptability, 41–43
Adaptive problems, 201–202
Affective questions, 96
Ally, Shamir, 205; biography, 247
Amgen, 214–215
Analytical questions, 96
Anderson, Neal, 165
Andracchi, Frank, 77–78; biography, 247; on conflict management, 54; on problem solving, 199–200
Anheuser-Busch, 131, 227
Answer dependency, 143–145
Answer-driven organizations, 31–32
Appreciative inquiry, 113
Association for the Blind and Visually Impaired—Goodwill Industries, 235
Austin, James, 228

B

Badaracco, Joseph, 54, 55, 57
Bay of Pigs invasion, 17–18
Bertucci Watch Company, 205
Best-in-class questions, 156
Biehl, Bobb, 39
Blanchard, Ken, 230
Bossing, vs. coaching, 109
Boston Red Sox, 20
Bristol-Myers-Squibb, 131
Busch, August, III, 130–131

C

Canadian Imperial Bank of Commerce (CIBC), 220
Carew, Jeff, 12–13, 78; biography, 248; on innovation, 47; on learning, 164–165; on listening, 121; on the role of questions in organizational learning, 35–36; on why questions, 93–94
Cargill's Malt Americas, 221
Carkhuff, Roger, 156
Carnegie, Dale, 22
Center for Creative Leadership, 132
Challenger spacecraft, explosion of, 16
Champy, James, 161
Change, leading organizational change, 232–235
Charoux, Eric: biography, 248; on conflict management, 194; on organizational change, 232–233; on questioning culture, 143
Cheng, Lily, 161–162, 217

Cheng, Peter, 154–155, 161–162, 217;
  biography, 248
Cisco, 227
Clarifying questions, 96, 191
Closed questions, 98–99
Coaching: action learning, 258–259,
  266–270; adopting a learning attitude,
  110; vs. bossing, 109; establishing a
  coaching relationship with direct
  reports, 156–159; leading teams as a
  coach-questioner, 178–186
Coffman, Vance, 37–38
Cohen, Gary, 13–14, 146
Coleman, Mike: on avoiding asking
  questions, 66; biography, 248; on
  following up, 126; on impact of
  questions on leaders, 240; on mindset
  for asking questions, 105; on teamwork,
  45–46
Collins, Jim, 20, 24, 139; Level 5 leaders,
  57
Commitment, 187; to learn and develop,
  56–57
Communication, 52–53
Community, 187; questions for,
  227–229
Confidence, 211
Conflict management, 53–54; questions
  that help you manage team conflict,
  193–196
Contemplation in action, 71
Corporate culture, 74–77
Corporate values, 229
Courage, 66
Culture. *See* answer-driven organizations;
  corporate culture; questioning culture
Customers, questions for, 220–223

D
DCDM Business School, 232–233
Decision making, and a questioning
  culture, 38–41
Deep listening, 211. See also listening
Deep questioning, 209–210
Dell, Michael, 27–28, 32
Dialogue, 135–137; questioning via,
  207–208
Disaster prevention, day-to-day,
  18–19
Disempowering questions, 84–86, 153
Disputes, using questions to handle,
  36
Double-loop learning, 40

Drucker, Peter, 22–23, 27, 219; on
  leadership, 230; on listening, 121
DuPont, 131–132, 139, 227

E
Eden, Douglas, 23–24, 43; biography,
  248–249; on customers, 221; on goals,
  166; on listening, 52; on organizational
  change, 236
Edmondson, Ron, 151–152; biography,
  249
Effective executives, nine practices of,
  22–23
Empathy, 141
Empowering employees, 43–44
Empowering questions, 84–86, 153
Encouraging open discussion and debate,
  186–188
Encouraging people to ask and respond to
  questions, 171–172
ETDT (eliminate the dumb things), 77
Explorative questions, 95

F
Failure to ask questions, 20–22
Family Health Council of Central
  Pennsylvania, 234–235
Fear, 64–68
Feedback, 170–171. *See also* performance
  appraisals
Finding great questions, 101–102
Finkelstein, Sidney, 20, 21; on corporate
  culture, 75
The 5 Elements of Effective Thinking
  (Burger and Starbird), 204
Flexibility, 50–52
Following up, 125–126
Ford Motor Company, 227
Fostering reflection and learning,
  159–162
Framing questions, 110–114
Fresh questions, 96, 173

G
Gaillard, Jean-Paul, 163–164, 204–205;
  biography, 249
Goals, 230
Goldberg, Marilee, 162; on empowering
  questions, 86; on strategy, 230–231
Goldsmith, Marshall, 28–29, 126; on
  encouraging people to ask and respond
  to questions, 171–172
Good to Great (Collins), 20, 57

Groupthink, 17–18
GROW model, 182

H

Halloran, Jean, on empowering others, 86
Hamel, Gary, 163
Hammer, Michael, 219
Harbison, John R., 225
Harper, Mark: on benefits of a questioning
culture, 40; biography, 249; on
coaching, 157; on encouraging action
and innovation, 162–163; on great
questions, 88; on questioning culture,
144–145, 147; on skills in asking
questions, 73; on teams, 181–182, 183;
on using questions to gain new
perspectives, 36–37
Heimbold, Charles, 131
Helping (Schein), 241
Hesse, Herman, 268
Hesselbein, Frances, 123, 235
Hewlett-Packard Laboratories, 231
Hoffman, Robert, 3, 79; biography, 249;
on building relationships, 160; on
listening, 122–123; on problem solving,
203–204, 208; on questioning
culture, 51
Holliday, Chad, 2, 81, 188; biography,
249–250; on impatience, 68–69; on
modeling the way, 131–132; on
opportunity to ask questions, 139; on
questioning stakeholders, 227; on why
questions, 95
Hopf, Gidget, 12; biography, 250; on
coaching, 157–158; on opportunity to
ask questions, 140; on strategy, 235; on
using questions as a reality check, 186
How to Win Friends and Influence People
(Carnegie), 22

I

Iceberg tips, 123
Image, 230
Individual benefits of a questioning
culture, 48; better listening and
communication, 52–53; conflict
management, 53–54; greater
self-awareness, 48–50; greater
understanding and skills in
organizational and political realities,
55–56; self-confidence, openness, and
flexibility, 50–52; stronger commitment
to learn and develop, 56–57; stronger
leadership, 57–58

Innovation, 47–48; encouraging, 162–165
The Innovative Leader (Sloane), 241–242
Inquiry Institute, 272
Inquiry leadership: practicing, 242–243.
See also questioning leaders
Iorio, Pam, 76; biography, 250; on great
questions, 88–89

J

Janis, Irving, 17
Journey to the East (Hesse), 268
Judger mindset: defined, 104; vs. learner
mindset, 101–108; questions asked
from, 108
Just Ask Leadership (Cohen), 146
Kanter, Rosabeth Moss, 234
Kennedy, John F., 17–18, 243
Kennedy, Robert, 18
Kliman, Stuart, 226–227
Knowling, Robert, Jr., 231–232
Kotter, John, 22, 232, 239

L

Lantz, Gayle, on great questions, 90
Laughlin, Tom, 79; biography, 250; on
building relationships, 158–159
Leaders: becoming a leader who asks
questions, 242–243; creating
motivation and environment to
challenge the status quo, 133–137;
great questions defining great leaders,
27–29; impact of questions on,
240–242; making sure values and
processes don't conflict with questions,
137–139; vs. managers, 22; modeling
the way, 130–133; optimizing the
opportunities to ask questions,
139–140; providing training in
questioning, 142–143; rewarding and
appreciating questioners, 141–142; role
in creating a questioning culture, 130;
slowing the pace and the pressure, 142;
traditional and coaching leaders'
behavior and legacies, 179–181; what
happens when leaders don't ask
questions, 14–18
Leadership, 57–58; leading with questions
in the 21st century, 243–244
Leading questions, 100
Leading Quietly (Badaracco), 54, 55
Leading with Questions
Academy/PACE-OD, 272
Leading with questions, research on
leaders who lead with questions, 4–6

Leading with Questions website/blog, 272–273
Learner mindset: adopting, 108–110; defined, 104; vs. judger mindset, 101–108; questions asked from, 107–108
Learning, fostering, 159–162
Learning orientation, 211
Lencioni, Patrick, 186
Lendemann, Rick, biography, 250–251
Listening, 52–53; deep listening, 211; and showing interest in the response, 120–125; sincere listening and learning, 126–127
Loyalty, 137, 223

M

Mahfouz, Naguib, 241
Managers, vs. leaders, 22
Managing key employee interactions, 165–173
Marshall Space Center, 16
Maryland Chemical Company, 222
Mead, Margaret, 177
Meetings, energizing team meetings, 188–190
Merchant, Nilofer, 199
Milchling, Suzanne, 80; on avoiding asking questions, 67; biography, 251; on great questions, 89–90; on probing questions, 96–97; on questioning style, 153–154
Mill, John Stuart, 23, 186
Milliken, 222
Mindset for asking questions, judger vs. learner, 101–108
Mission, 230
Mitroff, Ian, 40
Mittelstaedt, Robert E., 15–16
Moon, Kook-Hyun, biography, 251
Morale, 185
Morris, John, 56–57, 80
Morton Thiokol, Inc. (MTI), 16
Motivating employees, 43–44
Motivation, creating, 133–137
Motorola, 220
Multiple questions, 100

N

NASA, 16
New employees, 172–173

O

On Liberty (Mill), 186
Open-ended questions, 91–93, 95–97, 191; working with, 97–98
Openness, 50–52
Organizational awareness, 55–56
Organizational benefits of a questioning culture: enhanced innovation, 47–48; greater adaptability and acceptance of organizational change, 41–43; improved decision making and problem solving, 38–41; motivating and empowering employees, 43–44; overview, 34–38; stronger teamwork, 44–46
Ostland, Charles, 192–193; biography, 251; on self-reflection, 69

P

Panas, Jerold, 152
Parker, Mike, 21–22
Partlow, Jeanette, 222; biography, 251; on performance appraisals, 169
Partners, questions for, 224–227
Pekar, Peter, Jr., 225
Performance appraisals, 167–169. See also feedback
Peters, Tom, on teams, 177
Peterson, Donald, 23
Pfizer, 203–204, 225
Planning, questions for, 165–167
Power Questions (Sobel and Panas), 152
Probing questions, 96–97, 192
Problem solving: enabling a group to ask questions when problem solving, 210–211; gaining an understanding of the real problem through questions, 202–204; improving questions while, 211–212; overview, 199–200; and a questioning culture, 38–41; questions at various stages of, 206–210; questions for breakthrough problem solving, 204–205; technical and adaptive problems, 200–202
Purpose, 230

Q

Questioning and Teaching (Dillon), 116
Questioning culture: better listening and communication, 52–53; conflict management, 53–54; defined, 32–34; enhanced innovation, 47–48; greater adaptability and acceptance of

organizational change, 41–43; greater self-awareness, 48–50; greater understanding and skills in organizational and political realities, 55–56; hallmarks of, 34; handling resistance to, 143–147; improved decision making and problem solving, 38–41; individual benefits of, 48; leader's role in creating, 130; motivating and empowering employees, 43–44; organizational benefits of, 34–38; self-confidence, openness, and flexibility, 50–52; stronger commitment to learn and develop, 56–57; stronger leadership, 57–58; stronger teamwork, 44–46

Questioning leaders, 256, 261–263

Questions: affective questions, 96; analytical questions, 96; clarifying questions, 96, 191; closed questions, 98–99; for details, 191; encouraging people to ask and respond to questions, 171–172; explorative questions, 95; finding great questions, 101–102; framing, 110–114; fresh questions, 96, 173; great questions defining great leaders, 27–29; leading questions, 100; multiple questions, 100; for new employees, 172–173; open-ended questions, 91–93, 95–98, 191; during performance appraisals, 167–169; for planning and setting objectives, 165–167; probing questions, 96–97, 192; reflective questions, 96; roots of great questions, 86–90; steps in the questioning process, 114–126; stimulating questions, 192; summarizing questions, 192; that create connections, 96; that disempower, 3; that empower or disempower, 84–86; that manipulate, 3–4; timing for, 114; types of effective questions, 91–99; as the ultimate leadership tool, 22–27; unhelpful questions, 100; what happens when leaders don't ask questions, 14–18; why questions, 93–95. *See also* failure to ask questions; trouble asking questions

Quiet leadership, 54

R

Rajab, Effendy Mohamed, 36; on being more politically sensitive, 55; biography, 251–252; on framing

questions, 112; on open-ended questions, 92; on perspective, 71–72

Reality, facing, 20–22

Reality testing, 201–202

Reflection, fostering, 159–162

Reflective questions, 96

Relationships: establishing a coaching relationship with direct reports, 156–159; that empower, 152–156

Research, on leaders who lead with questions, 4–6

Resources, 271–273

Responsibility, sharing, 196

Revans, Reg, 87, 255

Rewarding and appreciating questioners, 141–142

Rimanoczy, Isabel, 2; biography, 252; on framing questions, 112–113; on leadership, 165

Rock, David, 70–71, 120, 142; biography, 252

Rogers, Carl, 156

Russell, Bertrand, 51–52

S

Schein, Edgar, 132–133, 147, 241

Schlesinger, Arthur, 17–18

Schmidt, Eric, 58

Self-awareness, 48–50, 159–160

Self-confidence, 50–52

Self-directedness, 210–211

Senge, Peter: on finding great questions, 101–102; on teams, 177

Sets. *See* action learning groups

78 Important Questions Every Leader Should Ask and Answer (Clarke-Epstein), 222–223

Shared values, 33

Sharer, Kevin, 214–215

Single-loop learning, 40

Sloane, Paul, 241–242

Slowing the pace and the pressure, 142

Smart Thinking for Crazy Times (Mitroff), 40

Smyk, David: biography, 252; on decision making and problem solving, 38–39; on framing questions, 111; on morale, 184–185; on performance appraisals, 169

Sobel, Andrew, 152

Stakeholders, 218–219; community, 227–229; customers, 220–223; vendors and partners, 224–227

Steps in the questioning process, 114; asking your questions, 116–120; breaking the ice, 114–115; following up, 125–126; listening and showing interest in the response, 120–125; setting the stage, 115–116

Stewart, Cindy, 18–19, 63, 65, 80; biography, 252–253; on following up, 125–126; on leading questions, 117; on organizational change, 234–235

Stice, Mike, 14; biography, 253; on framing questions, 113–114; on open-ended questions, 160; on using questions to handle organizational disputes, 36

Stimulating questions, 192

Strategic intent, 77

Strategy: developing strategic vision and values, 229–232; leading organizational change, 232–235; questioning stakeholders outside the organization, 218–229; using questions to bring a fresh perspective, 214–218

Summarizing questions, 192

Sydänmaanlakka, Pentti, 2; biography, 253; on feedback, 170–171; on innovation, 47; on leadership, 58, 164; on questioning culture, 33

The System of Logic (Mill), 23

T

Teams: encouraging open discussion and debate, 186–188; energizing team meetings, 188–190; goals of team-building, 184–186; helping the team overcome obstacles, 190–193; leading as a coach-questioner, 178–186; overview, 177–178; questions that help you manage team conflict, 193–196; sharing responsibility, 196. See also action learning groups

Teamwork, 44–46

Technical problems, 200–201

Telling dependency, 143, 145–147

Theories in use, 161

Thornhill, Mark, 129; biography, 253–254; on leadership, 57; on questioning culture, 135

Thoughtful questioning, 210

Tichy, Noel, 21

Tiede, Bob, 272–273

Timing questions, 114

Titanic, sinking of, 15–16

Toyota, 227

Training in questioning, 142–143

Transformative learning, 159

Triple-loop learning, 40

Trouble asking questions, 63–64; being in a rush, 68–72; confronting discomfort with questions, 77–81; corporate cultures discouraging questions, 74–77; desire to protect ourselves, 64–68; lack of skills in asking questions, 72–74

U

Ultimate empowerment tool, 22

Unhelpful questions, 100

USS Benfold, 25–27

V

Vaill, Peter, 163

Values, 230; asking value-related questions, 156; corporate values, 229; developing strategic vision and values, 229–232; making sure values and processes don't conflict with questions, 137

Vendors, questions for, 224–227

W

Walt Disney World (WDW), 215–216

Warner-Lambert, 203–204

Warrier, Jayan, 173–174; biography, 254; on conflict management, 195

Welch, Jack, 21, 32

Wheatley, Margaret, 43; on dialogue, 136–137; on leadership, 133; on opportunity to ask questions, 139–140; on teams, 177; on teamwork, 46

Whitemore, John, 182

White-space opportunities, 76–77

Whitt, Sue: biography, 254; on developing a coaching relationship, 109–110; on learning, 56; on performance appraisals, 168; on questioning vendors, 225; on teams, 182–183; on teamwork, 44–45

Why questions, 93–95

Why Smart Executives Fail (Finkelstein), 20, 75

Will Your Next Mistake Be Fatal?
  (Mittelstaedt), 15–16
Winning (Welch), 32
Wooden, John, 118
World Institute for Action Learning
  (WIAL), 271
Worthington Steel, 220
Wurtzel, Alan, 145

Y

Yawkey, Tom, 20

Z

"Zombie Businesses", 20–21
Zombies, 21